NOTRE DAME AND IRELAND

Published by Keough Naughton Notre Dame Centre Dublin.

O'Connell House
58 Merrion Square
Dublin 2
Ireland.

ISBN 978-0-9573534-0-4

Designed by Vermillion: www.vermilliondesign.com
Printed in Ireland by Colorman

NOTRE DAME AND IRELAND

A DUBLIN PERSPECTIVE

Edited by Kevin Whelan
Photography by Eimear Clowry

EDITORIAL COLLECTIVE
Lisa Caulfield, Eimear Clowry, Andrew Hoyt, Joe Stranix, Courtney Wahle, Kevin Whelan

ACKNOWLEDGEMENTS

Rev. John Jenkins, CSC, President of the University of Notre Dame: Thomas Burish, Provost: Don and Mickie Keough: Martin and Carmel Naughton: Fergal and Rachael Naughton: Seamus Heaney: the Hon. Mr. Justice Adrian Hardiman: Mary McAleese: Trinity College Dublin, especially Jane Ohlmeyer: Abbey Theatre, especially Oonagh Desire: Royal Irish Academy, especially Siobhán Fitzpatrick: Scott Tallon Walker, especially David Flannery: Notre Dame colleagues Patrick Griffin, Declan Kiberd, Seamus Deane, Bob Schmuhl, Aédin Clements, Deb Rotman, John Hannan and Sean O'Brien: Dublin Domers, Greer Hannan, Ginna Dybic, Elizabeth Moore, Betsy McGovern, Chris Rehagen, Emilee Booth Chapman and Diana Gutierrez: the staff of the Keough Naughton Notre Dame Centre Dublin, Louise Marren, Rachel McEvoy and Aoife Drinan: John Hannan, Mike Lowe, Elizabeth Hogan (Photography Archive, ND), Steve Warner (Folk Choir): Fr Peyton Centre (Attymass), especially Rev. James Phalan, C.S.C. and Rev. Steve Gibson, C.S.C.: Marie O'Brien; Susan Aldrich: Ellen Skerrett: Bébhinn Whelan and Anne Kearney.

A particular thanks to Vermillion, Irish design leaders, especially Anne Brady and Kevin Dunne.

Photo credits: Eoghan Kavanagh, Skyline Gallery, Kenmare: Edmund Ross: Mary Lesch and The Mary and John Lesch Family Collection: Matt Cashore (ND): Máire Devlin: Brendan Dunford: Molly Byrne: Greer Hannan: Siomha Moore: Carolyn Bates: Perry McIntyre: Susan Kennedy (Irish Photo Archive): Aoife Drinan: Trinity College Dublin: Courtney Wahle: Populous, Scott Tallon Walker & Donal Murphy: Ó Buachalla family: Jane Bown: Monica Bushman: Andrew Hoyt: Ryan Greenberg: Elena Rodriguez: Luke Klopp: Colleen McCartney: Kate Nolan: Louise Marren: Victor Patterson: Elizabeth Moore: Lisa Caulfield.

CONTENTS

engagement, and over eighty percent of students will volunteer during their time at ND, with many also engaging in post-graduate service.

The novelist Harper Lee, after receiving an honorary doctorate from the University, wrote to Notre Dame's president, Rev. John Jenkins, CSC: 'Notre Dame is unlike any American university I have seen – and I have seen quite a few. In addition to its ranking for academic excellence, the place seems to proclaim a sense of purpose in life, lacking in other institutions. . . . You are unique'.

That sense of purpose crosses international boundaries, as students routinely travel abroad for their studies, service and research, and the University constantly aims to enhance the international reach of its scholarly endeavours. In Ireland, it partners with two fine institutions, Trinity College and University College Dublin, fruitful collaborations that allow Notre Dame to deepen and extend its international presence.

These partnerships are but one example of how, as the University has grown and developed, Notre Dame has continued to cherish its connection to Ireland and the Irish people. Tracing the enduring bond between Notre Dame and the Emerald Isle, from its foundation in 1842 through the resurgence in Irish Studies in the 1990s to the current flourishing state of the University's involvement with Ireland, this book is a celebration of and reflection upon this proud heritage.

Thomas G. Burish
Provost, University of Notre Dame

The Golden Dome: University of Notre Dame

Máire Devlin (ND Dublin Fall 09) captures the spirit of the Dublin programme in her photograph 'Ireland in the palm of my hand'. The Irish tricolour – green, white and gold – is replicated in pebbles taken from the stream at Glendalough.

On Derrynane Beach, County Kerry, Spring 2010

SPIRIT OF THE DUBLIN PROGRAMME

I

CHAPTER

SPIRIT OF THE DUBLIN PROGRAMME

A natural outgrowth of Notre Dame's Irish-American background was to establish an Irish presence. In 1998, this was realised through the establishment of the Keough Notre Dame Centre (renamed the Keough Naughton Centre in 2006). The centre was initially based in Newman House, courtesy of a partnership agreement with University College Dublin. Newman House is indelibly associated with John Henry Cardinal Newman, the galvanising force in founding the Catholic University there in 1852. It was for this Dublin institution that he wrote *The Idea of a University*, whose limpid prose and elegant formulation still provides the template for a university imbued with Catholic principles but animated by intellectual ambition. In 2012, when the Cambridge don, Stefan Collini, answers the question posed in his book *What are universities for?*, it is still to Newman that he turns to defend the purity of intellectual enquiry as the animating heart of any great university. Because Notre Dame embodies Newman's vision of blending faith and intellect, locating the Dublin Programme in Newman House was a form of home coming, a return to the living roots of the Notre Dame tradition.

Newman House on Stephen's Green. Through this door of the Catholic University passed such figures as James Joyce, Gerard Manley Hopkins and Patrick Pearse. Newman House is the original home of what became University College Dublin.

The 1990s was the decade when the University of Notre Dame ramped up its globalisation initiatives in earnest. As a result, it now routinely sends over half of the student body to study in other countries. This figure places Notre Dame among the top ten of American research universities.

With the university leadership driving it on, Notre Dame quickly became a powerhouse of international studies globally. Over one thousand of its students have studied at Trinity College Dublin and University College Dublin, with both of whom ND has mutually enriching partnerships. From a Notre Dame perspective, these links with our Irish partner universities have been crucial to embedding us in Ireland.

ND operates a trilateral partnership with University College Dublin and Trinity College Dublin. This is not a conventional study abroad programme. Our students enjoy a genuine immersion experience by living with Irish students in on-campus accommodation and taking courses at their host institutions. Because of our partnership with the Irish universities, we can cater for a much wider array of student majors than in conventional international programme, including Arts and Letters, Business, Science and Engineering. The result has been a tremendous explosion of undergraduate interest across a wide spectrum – literature, history, art, business, anthropology, archaeology, politics, Northern Ireland, Irish language, biology, chemistry, biochemistry, physics, chemical engineering, civil engineering, electrical engineering, mechanical engineering. We generally have ten full year students at Trinity College, and thirty-five semester students at University College Dublin, as well as forty in our postgraduate Irish Seminar, twenty-five in our Dublin Summer Programme, and another ten in summer internships. Immersed full time at these two fine Irish universities, our

Trinity College Dublin was founded in 1592. ND students based here live facing Front Square – one of the finest assemblages of eighteenth-century university buildings anywhere in the world. Trinity College is ranked among the top 50 universities globally.

students live, study and socialise with the other students. Judging by their letters of application, our cohort often have an Irish connection: the Irish grandmother remains a powerful force in American life. But they by no means come exclusively from Irish-American backgrounds: our undergraduate participants have come from Australia, Canada, China, Columbia, France, Germany, Honduras, Korea, Mexico, Paraguay, South Korea, and even Ireland!

As an immersed programme, we place a central emphasis on informal and experiential learning: our students discover a great deal in late night discussions about life, politics, culture, and the poor quality of Irish showers. Here too for the first time, they discover what it means to be an American; the moment they open their mouths here, they are tagged as 'American' – something that never happens to them in South Bend – because only other people have 'accents'. That experience encourages them to become self-conscious about being American; it becomes a useful reflective tool for them in evaluating their own lives, and in understanding how America is viewed in the contemporary world.

It is not that this encounter changes them, but that it stimulates them to articulate in a clearer way what has hitherto been ill-defined or taken-for-granted. The very first challenge that we pose to our students when they arrive in Dublin is 'What does she of America know who only America knows'? Ironically, it can be here in Ireland that our students first discover what it means to be an American in the wider world. The last challenge that we pose to them is

Fieldtrips are an essential component in encouraging our students to engage with Ireland. Here they learn about Lemeneagh Castle in County Clare.

Giants Causeway, Undergraduate Programme, Spring 2010.

'Learning through the soles of your feet'. Students explore the prehistoric fort on Black Head in the Burren, with an enormous Irish sky towering above them. The mobility of the sky is one of the glories of the West of Ireland.

an intellectual one: to bring back what they have learned in Europe to the ND campus and to America. As we share an increasingly globalising world, we motivate our students to think hard about America's role in the wider sphere, and to understand that there is more than one way of being in the world – neither better or worse – just different.

Dublin, a young, vibrant, dynamic city, is now ranked easily within the ten best locations in the world for study abroad, so it is unsurprising that the Dublin programme attracts one of the strongest applicant pools of any of Notre Dame's many international programmes. Hundreds of students compete for the limited places. One result is the extraordinary calibre of the students that we accept: our Trinity College intake tend to have GPAs of between 3.8 and 4. A less pleasant aspect of our jobs is that we disappoint students (and their parents and grandparents!) when they do not get into the programme. We have to explain that what makes our programme attractive – its intimacy – is what also make us selective. We deliberately keep numbers below fifty, so that we can genuinely focus on getting to know each participant personally, and so that we can share varied experiences together. Under fifty students can fit on the same bus, or in our homes, or get tickets for a game or a play: our mantra has become 'Quantity eventually influences Quality'. Our preferred form of expanding the programme has been to extend the range of possibilities rather than just to increase the raw numbers.

Mark Twain once said that 'Travel is lethal to prejudice'. With Ireland around them, and Europe on their doorstep (nineteen European capitals lie within three hours flight time from Dublin), we encourage our students to marinate themselves in culture, art, architecture, literature, music, sport and politics. Speaking with our students, Don Keough once said that 'to make yourself interesting, you have to do interesting things and meet interesting people' and an international experience allows them to do just that. Our students demonstrate the courage to step outside their comfort zone, and the flexibility to adapt to a different educational system and culture. In the longer term, they are rewarded for accepting the challenge. We have found that having an international experience on their resumes enhances their likelihood of being admitted to elite American Graduate Schools, and of securing excellent jobs as companies increasingly favour candidates with international exposure.

We inhabit a world where T-shaped learning is increasingly salient. T-shaped students have a principal skill (the vertical leg of the T) but they also branch out (the horizontal bar of the T). They have deep expertise in one discipline but a broad knowledge base in others, and a wide range of cultural experience and passionate interests, including travel. These students possess the skills that companies increasingly seek. However, T-shaped learning can be inhibited in a narrowly disciplinary environment. Universities must certainly excel in producing students who are 'deep' in their specific disciplines, but they must also increasingly engage them in broadening the top bar of the T. International study, internships, community-based learning, and experiential learning are all crucial to developing the skills necessary to flourish in the modern world, which is rapidly evolving away from traditional routine, top-down manufacturing-based models towards services-based economies. T-shaped people are the innovators, able to engage in the all-important lateral thinking that comes up with new thinking about old problems. An international study experience is a pre-eminent way to encourage T-shaped skills – critical thinking, creativity, path-finding, innovation, leadership, global awareness and technological literacy. Study Abroad is by definition an exercise in T-shaped learning: developing enthusiasm and expertise about different topics, and becoming more flexible, more empathetic, more engaged with the wider world.

In Dublin, we emphasise to our students that living abroad is an opportunity for extraordinary intellectual but also personal growth, that will stand them in good stead in their future lives. They must meet the multiple challenges of living abroad: for some, it can be chilly initially, away from the warm cocoon of the ND campus. We always stress that missing family and friends is the most natural thing in the world, that there will be moments of vulnerability, discouragement and loneliness, and that not everything will go smoothly. But we also stress that it is not what happens to you that defines you but how you respond to it. We are constantly amazed at how well our students rise to the challenge; their resilience, good-humour, competence and faith carry them through, even in stressful situations. When they look back on their time in Ireland, every student recognises that they grew and matured here, as they faced the pitfalls as well as the opportunities of living abroad.

In Dublin, we seek to build a sense of community that is based on a shared journey and a complementarity of gifts – 'unique but united' is another of our mantras. We believe that each student is called to an excellence that is not based on competition with others, or an unrelenting focus on minute differences in GPA. Each of us has our unique range of gifts

Dublin's Beckett Bridge (2009), by the Spanish architect Santiago Calatrava. The bridge, resembling a harp on it side, has created an iconic portal for the modern city. Dublin is designated as a UNESCO City of Literature, so it is appropriate that the bridge is named in honour of the dramatist Samuel Beckett (1906–1989).

and our unique limits, that open a personal life journey that is distinct from everyone else's. We seek to elicit excellence but not in a selfish way that inhibits our capacity to rejoice in the gifts, graces and accomplishments of others. Our students are augmented by each others' talents rather than being diminished by them. Recognising this complementarity allows them to contribute to the common good at their points of strength, as well as experiencing their *limits* as well as their gifts as gracious. It is our limits that free us to more fully appreciate family, friendship and fellowship.

Once all of us – students, faculty, staff – continually reorient ourselves to face outwards as well as inwards, we can build a community based around awareness of what we can do to enhance the lives and spirits of those journeying with us. Our motto is derived from the Irish proverb 'Is ar scáth a chéile a mhaireann na daoine' (literally, 'It is in the shadow of each other that people endure', metaphorically, 'We all flourish in community'). We remind our students to be aware at all times that they represent their family, their university, and their country. The Dublin Notre Dame community is anchored in the concepts of trust and responsibility, a constant awareness of what the American poet Frank Bidart meant when he said: 'The love I have known is the love of two people staring not at each other, but in the same direction'. We stress that this is their programme, not ours; that they, not us, are Notre Dame in Dublin; that we are nothing without our students. O'Connell House is theirs before it is ours, and we expect that anyone who comes through our blue door is always greeted by a cheery word, a smile, or a cup of tea.

As they leave, our participants know that they can face the future confidently. An international study experience offers a valuable halfway house between the sheltered university and the exposed work environment. It also offers an incentive to life-long learning, not just in its university segment. Their engagement with Irish and European culture nourishes their sense of beauty and wonder as they can come up close and personal with great paintings, great books, great films, great architecture, great cities and great sporting occasions. Their culinary ambitions broaden, and their level of apprehension around foreign travel drops dramatically. International study fosters an openness to the world and to new things: our students learn above all that diversity is a healthy thing, culturally as well as environmentally.

Walking through the narrow streets of West Belfast, Spring 2009.

A learning environment should also be a fun environment. Dublin Summer Programme 2012 participants Mikey Keough and Nate Bombardier in Iveagh Gardens.

William Butler Yeats once said that 'Education is not the filling of a pail, but the lighting of a fire'. Good educators are not 'content-providers' but igniters. They prioritise, not the imparting of information, but the finding of ways to connect with the passions that each student has, and giving that student permission to express that passion. A good teacher is a mentor, an encourager of gifts, a lighter of fires. That is our principal challenge here in Dublin – to help our students become the person they want to be, to embody the Notre Dame blend of faith and intellect, and to seek to lead lives of moral purpose and conviction.

Our students always thank us as they leave, but actually it us who should be thanking them. They think they learn from us but really we learn from them – they are a brain-gain rather than a brain-drain for Ireland. Having had the pleasure of getting to know over one thousand of them well, we can say that Notre Dame students make us so proud both of them and for them. They embody everything that we could wish for in young people: optimism, good humour, idealism, fun, a willingness to stretch themselves, a desire to serve others, to learn, and to live their faith in their daily lives. Engaging with these wonderful young people renews our faith in the future of the world: they are the best antidote to cynicism or jadedness. Notre Dame's finest, they give us so much more than we can ever give them. They make every day a good day in O'Connell House.

The next parish is America. Tim Masterton looking out from the Aran cliffs.

Spring 2012 students explore in Glendalough. Finding your balance is a central challenge during study abroad.

From the Heart: Courtney Wahle, Dublin Spring 2005

I remember the first time I arrived in Dublin on that dark January morning. My flight from Boston was the first of many to touch down in the early hours, carrying sleep-deprived Notre Dame students eager to begin their adventure abroad. But with only one other student on my flight and hours before the next plane landed, my anxiety slowly mounted and I felt I would do anything for a hot cup of tea.

It was as I began to question spending five months away from everything I knew when I was greeted by Katie Murphy and Kevin Whelan of the Dublin Programme. I remember wondering how they possibly could have spotted me in that crowded airport – even with those unmistakable, oversized luggage bags that screamed 'Study Abroad student from America'. The memory of that moment still brings a smile to my face. Here I was, thousands of miles away from the Golden Dome. And yet, when I least expected it, Notre Dame had found me on this tiny speck of green across the Atlantic.

It has been seven years since I first experienced the proverbial Irish 'céad míle fáilte', and upon graduation in Spring 2006 it became my privilege to welcome ND students to Ireland as the Programme Co-ordinator of the Dublin Centre. During my three years working for the Dublin Programme, one of my favorite moments was meeting the students as they emerged uncertainly from the automatic doors at Dublin Airport. When my eyes first caught sight of those weary yet expectant faces, I was reminded all over again of why my presence was so important. Their feeling welcome in a foreign country was the gateway to their entire study abroad experience – the first of many encounters that they would have during their search for the new, strange, and wonderful things that come from forming a new Notre Dame family, and, together, turning O'Connell House into a home.

It is through the countless opportunities offered through the Dublin programme that ND students are able to immerse themselves in the very best of what Ireland has to offer. From the classrooms of Trinity College and University College Dublin, to educational trips ranging from the majestic Cliffs of Moher in the West to the geological geometry of the Giant's Causeway in the North, our students absorb the stunning sights, rich smells, and captivating Irish songs that stir the soul and leave their stamp on the mind. We encourage them to engage in conversation with the people they encounter, to understand and appreciate the differences between America and Ireland, and to be open to the ever-present chance to learn something new. By the end of the term, our students inevitably find time tugging at their coattails. As they board the plane back to America, however, they say goodbye to Dublin knowing that their lives have been enriched among new friends that they will always remember in a country that they will not soon forget.

To a sophomore at Notre Dame, the idea of studying abroad can seem like an unimaginable journey and a daunting risk to take, especially for one who is considering spending the Fall months away from ND Stadium. However, if you embrace the challenge, remain open to the experience, and have the courage to be the author of your own story, you will find a house with a blue door in a bustling city on a breathtakingly beautiful island that is waiting for you, too, to call it home.

Aviva Stadium Dublin. Notre Dame v. Navy, 1 September 2012.

THE FOUNDERS: DON KEOUGH AND MARTIN NAUGHTON

2

CHAPTER

DON KEOUGH AND MARTIN NAUGHTON: THE FOUNDERS

Martin Naughton and Don Keough. 'People who are destined to meet will do so, apparently by chance, when the time is right'(Ralph Waldo Emerson).

DON KEOUGH

It was a proud moment for Don Keough, his wife Mickie, their six children, eighteen grandchildren, hundreds of friends, and thousands of well-wishers when he became an Irish citizen in 2007. The surname Mac Eochaidh, anglicised as Keogh, Kehoe or Keough, originated in County Wexford, where the family were the hereditary bards to the Kavanaghs, ancient Kings of Leinster. For centuries, the Keoughs maintained a famous bardic school at Pallas near Gorey in north Wexford. Bards were the senior intellectuals in the Gaelic cultural system – teachers, mentors, trusted advisors, custodians of traditions and values, historians and poets always, spin-doctors as required.

The pronunciation of the name Mac Eochaidh has gone through many variations – in fact, the 'Keough' version is closer to the original Irish form in both orthography and sound. When families bearing this name landed at Ellis Island, immigration officials wrote down what they heard and therefore it is not at all surprising that Keough became the official version, since that is how the Irish pronunciation of the name sounded to an American ear.

Don's great-grandfather Michael Keough left County Wexford in the 1840s during the Famine and arrived in America, where he married Hannah, then only eighteen years old. This was a love-match and the courageous young newly-weds became sodbusters, farmers and ranchers settled on the prairies of north-west Iowa. Don was born here in the heart of the mid-west in 1926. His people were cattlemen. He later moved to Omaha, Nebraska, where among his neighbours was Warren Buffet, who became his life-long friend. After serving in the American Navy in World War II, Don entered university on the G. I. Bill. His first career was as a radio talk-show host in Omaha, working with the legendary Johnny Carson. Don joined Coca-Cola in 1965, and moved rapidly up through the ranks to become its COO in 1981. He retired as president, director and chairman of Coca-Cola Enterprises in 1993, when he was appointed advisor to the board. He was re-elected to the Board in 2003 and still serves in that capacity.

The rise of the Keough family from the prairies of the Mid-West to the pinnacle of Wall Street is the story in microcosm of Irish-America. If the immigrant Michael Keough could see his great-grandson today, what would he think? He would recognise in Don the classic Irish immigrant values of commitment to family and faith, community and country, hard work, determination, good humour, lack of pretentiousness, unflagging energy, an ability to adapt to fresh challenges, and an expectation that people should wear out, not rust out. The poet Robert Frost said of America: 'Our most precious heritage is what we haven't in our possession – what we haven't made, and so have still to make'. Don Keough embodies the possibility of America, its dynamism, its optimism and its can-do spirit.

A media storm erupted in Ireland in 2007 over the playing of the 'foreign games' of rugby and soccer at Croke Park, the shrine to the indigenous games of Gaelic football and hurling. However, Notre Dame had already played an American football game there in 1996, a tangible expression of its reconnection with Ireland, an effort in which Don Keough was the driving force. A vigorous and visionary presence in American life for over half a century, Don Keough has also been a dynamic catalyst in Irish-America, supporting Irish business, education and culture. His journey from the golden wheat fields of the American prairies to the Golden Dome of Notre Dame, and then on to the green fields of Ireland, has been a huge part of Don's life.

He has always stressed that 'Success is not a destination, it's a journey'. Unquestionably, a primary vehicle for his links with Ireland is his longstanding involvement with the University of Notre Dame. Don was elected a trustee in 1978, eventually serving as chairman of the University's Board, before becoming a Life Trustee in 1997. He also received the Laetare Medal, one of Notre Dame's highest honours, in 1993.

The genius of Don Keough as chairman of the Board of Trustees, was to insist that the university should re-establish meaningful contact with Ireland, on the grounds that any of us, as individuals or as institutions, can only chart a true path to the future if we know exactly where we have come from. Don's priority was for those Notre Dame roots to stay planted strong and true, allowing the connection between America and Ireland to flourish. For Don, it has always been a case of following the Shakespearean motto: 'Suit the action to the word, the word to the action'. Accordingly, he not only advocated this reconnection: he made it happen. Don and Mickie generously endowed the Keough Center for Irish Studies (later the Keough-Naughton Institute) on the South Bend campus in 1993, under the leadership of the distinguished Irish man of letters Seamus Deane.

Keough recognised in Deane the vision to build a programme from scratch. Keough's guiding principle was to provide the canvas and the materials, and then to offer Deane the opportunity to paint his intellectual vision on this empty canvas. Deane, painting with gusto, stressed the importance of recruiting outstanding faculty, of strengthening the library holdings, of recognising the significance of the Irish language, of establishing a graduate programme, and of bringing a constant stream of distinguished speakers to campus. With Don's constant support, and with Chris Fox's energetic and capable backing, Irish Studies at Notre Dame became a world-class force surprisingly quickly.

It is typical of the prescience of Don Keough that he sought re-engagement with Ireland in the early 1990s. With impeccable timing, he pushed this move in 1993, just on the eve of the emergence of the Celtic Tiger and the Peace Process. Don was a constant sounding board and source of private counsel in the emergence of the Peace Process. When serving on the Taoiseach's Economic Advisory Council in the 1980s, his persuasive advocacy of a low Corporation Tax was key to ensuring that that bold policy initiative was taken, which many regard as pivotal to the emergence of the Celtic Tiger.

Don had already matched deeds to words in the 1970s, and

he was way ahead of the curve, as his was a strong voice in ensuring that Coca Cola opened its major European plant just outside Drogheda. More recently, he played an equally decisive role in landing a major Coca-Cola investment in Wexford, the home of his ancestors. Don also personally escorted scores of potential investors to Ireland, including his friends Bill Gates and Warren Buffet.

We hear much now about the application of business models to running a university, but Don had already applied the core of his business model to Irish Studies – identify the best people, recruit them aggressively, then get out of their way and let them get on with doing what needs to be done:

> When I am working with smart employees, I leave them alone; I give them room to move. Sure, I offer direction and intercede when I must, but I would rather let them develop in an independent fashion, free of a tight, controlling climate.

Since then, with Don driving it on, and backed to the hilt by Andy McKenna and Patrick McCartan (his friends and successors as Chair of the Trustees), Irish Studies at Notre Dame has gone from strength to strength, attracting a cohort of world-class scholars and establishing a thriving Graduate Programme. Don also forged a close partnership with Martin Naughton, insisting that only a balanced leadership would ensure the smooth functioning of an Irish-American entity.

In a 2006 ceremony involving President of Ireland Mary McAleese, the Keough Institute of Irish Studies and the Keough Notre Dame Centre in Dublin were renamed the Keough-Naughton Institute and the Keough Naughton Centre to reflect that vision. The Keough-Naughton Institute made history by establishing the first dedicated Irish Language and Literature Department in an American university, which achieved autonomy in 2010.

Provost Tom Burish and Don Keough, Dublin Castle 2008.

Don Keough did not just transform Irish Studies at the South Bend campus. With his backing, the University established the Keough Notre Dame Centre in 1998 at Newman House, and when the thriving Centre outgrew the space there, he and Martin Naughton helped Notre Dame to acquire historic O'Connell House on Merrion Square in 2002. This graceful Georgian house has enormous resonance as the former home of the distinguished Irish politician Daniel O'Connell.

From the beginning, Don Keough wisely insisted that Notre Dame could only forge a strong relationship with Ireland through a genuine engagement with Irish life, and through close collaboration with Irish partners. Thus, Notre Dame consciously chose not to offer a stand-alone programme, but to pursue an immersion model. Operating a trilateral partnership with University College Dublin and Trinity College, Notre Dame has sent over one thousand students to Ireland. It is a measure of Don's standing that both Notre Dame's partner universities have conferred honorary doctorates on him.

For our students, the quality of their educational and cultural experience has been so exceptional that they return to the US as cheerleaders for Ireland. In the long run, the Keough Naughton Notre Dame Centre in Dublin is laying sturdy foundations for a lasting partnership between our two countries, as these elite students gradually filter into leadership positions in American life. This constantly flowing stream of extraordinary young Americans, very well informed about contemporary Ireland, is nurturing a new generation of door openers for Ireland in the USA. Their positive Irish experience encourages them to become what Don Keough has always been – a lifelong and passionate advocate for Ireland. For Irish people, it is all the more important to maintain strong relationships in the long term, as the Irish emigrant stream has slowed.

As a small speck on the edge of Europe, we enjoy enormous profile and support in America, a national resource whose value we need to recognise more consistently. Don was amongst the earliest and most visionary of Irish-American

Don Keough with students Matt Anderson and Liz Miller, O'Connell House 2007.

leaders in nurturing these linkages. Notre Dame's connections with Dublin continue to energise the hyphen in Irish-America. Don himself exemplifies the trajectory of the Irish in America. They came in with nothing and rose to the top over several generations through hard work and the immigrant drive to succeed. Like Irish-America as a whole, Don broke through the glass ceiling of 'No Irish need apply' and he now serves on the boards of the Coca-Cola Company, Berkshire Hathaway, IAC/InterActive Corporation and Yankee Global Enterprises. He is currently chairman of the board of Allen & Company, a New York investment banking firm.

Don's maxims of leadership include the admonition to 'Stay Nervous'. One of the reasons why Don has occupied the centre of American life for so many decades is that he has never once rested on his very considerable laurels, and that he has instilled that same principle in those with whom he works. With Don around, none of us take anything for granted, as we continue to hear that insistent voice in our inner ears: 'Stay Nervous'. At the very pinnacle of the American business world, Don Keough remains a door opener and advocate for Ireland. He regards with enormous pleasure and pride the emergence of a renewed, confident and peaceful Ireland. He has said: 'Ireland is happening, it has earned a seat at the party. The thrill of my life is being a celebrant at that table'.

When Don and Mickie were awarded honorary Irish citizenship in 2007, a celebratory dinner was held at Slane Castle just under the legendary Hill of Slane. This was the place where Patrick drew on the ordinary materials

Don and Mickie Keough at Slane Castle, 2007.

of everyday life, like the shamrock, to bring the Christian message to the Irish people. Don, with the unwavering support of his wife Mickie, has followed in Patrick's footsteps by bringing together rather than separating his Catholicism and his formidable business acumen. Don and Mickie identified education as an integral part of the life of the church (this was also the Irish in them breaking out, as few cultures understand so well the fundamental role of education as a ladder of social advancement). The Keough way of living the faith has been to support education, thereby helping young people to discern, nurture and develop their gifts.

Looking back over his personal Irish journey, Don notes:

> The strength of Irish-America triggered a rebirth of intense interest in Irish affairs in the minds and hearts of thousands of American men and women who happily attached to their dossier and name the Irish-American designation. That is true in my own case – a modest reawakening of my Irish heritage and that of my wife, Mickie, became intense and lasting.

Don Keough has always stressed that, as we seek to enrich other people's lives, we really enrich ourselves, and that that motivation lies at the heart of all philanthropy. He has impacted hugely on thousands of lives, bringing wise counsel, high standards, good humour, vigour and momentum to strengthening the relationship between Ireland and America. Don Keough has a unique ability to make people feel valued and appreciated, to spur them on in their endeavours, and to ensure that they never stop striving for excellence. His stamp is all over the Irish Studies initiative at Notre Dame.

From the Heart: Don Keough speaking in the Mansion House 2008

Think back to the 1840s and from then on to the middle of the twentieth century, and the waves of Irish who kept sweeping into an America which gave them a little pride, a little hope and a little promise for the future.

The two countries remained linked by these Irish ancestors, who so influenced Notre Dame. A few decades ago, the thought of Irish Studies kept coming into my mind. Here was this place, Notre Dame, which was truly Irish. There wasn't a special place to study the Irishness of America and to study the place that so many of us came from. I wanted to work with the University of Notre Dame, to start an Irish Studies Programme. It's really amazing, isn't it, when you start something, when you push that forward, how far you can go.

Mickie and I were talking about it today…just think. Here we are in this incredible room, celebrating a thousand youngsters who had the privilege to come into this country, and to touch it, and to allow it to change their lives. Success has a thousand fathers; failure is an orphan. If you think about Notre Dame studies in Ireland, there's only one place you can go, and that's to the gentle Irishman, Martin Naughton.

I have a picture in my office of the two of us, and people often say to me, 'he looks like your brother', so I am now willing to acknowledge that I am, in fact, the older brother of Martin Naughton – on one condition: he has to ensure that I am the lead beneficiary in his will.

In the middle of the last century, paleontologist Teilhard de Chardin said 'we are in a constant state of becoming'. That is true of Notre Dame, it is true of Trinity, and it is true of University College Dublin, it is true of Ireland, but it is also true of America. Both of us have had this incredible economic boom, and you think it goes on forever, but no boom goes on forever.

I would encourage you as Irish men and women who are at this little inflection point in the history of Ireland, to remember that you are in fact in a state of becoming. It is exciting that success is not a straight line – it is like a stair step; you go up, and then there is a flat plateau. And maybe in both countries, we are on that same plateau.

And it is at that time when your real judgment, your real courage, your real wisdom, your real foresight and your real hope can take you to the next level. So I would hope that you would be excited about the new Ireland and what it is going to be. I cannot tell you what is going to happen, but I can tell you this – it is going to be more wonderful than yesterday because people like you are going to make that happen. I, for one, am proud to be an American, but I can tell you one last thing – I am also proud to be an Irishman.

MARTIN NAUGHTON

Martin Naughton, a distinguished Irish businessman, has played a pivotal role in nurturing Notre Dame's Irish programmes. He became a Trustee in 1991, and he was a founding member of the University's Ireland Council in 1999, of which he has served as Co-Chair (with Don Keough) since its inception. He received an honorary degree from Notre Dame in ceremonies marking the opening of the Keough Notre Dame Centre in Dublin in 1998 and he also holds honorary degrees from Trinity College Dublin, University College Dublin and Queen's University Belfast.

Martin's mother, Mary Ryan, hailed from Galway and his father Martin was from Belcarra in County Mayo, where the Naughton family gravestones lie in historic Ballintubber Abbey. The children were sent back West every summer to remind them that Mayo is where the family originated. Even though Martin was born in Dublin, and grew up in Dundalk, he was encouraged to think of himself as a West of Ireland person. His granny's window framed a magnificent view of Croagh Patrick and his most vivid childhood memory is of that window framing the mountain like a painting. There was great excitement in heading back West each year: a car ride across Ireland was an adventure then, as the driver navigated by following the telegraph poles.

Like many Irish families, especially those from the West of Ireland, the Naughtons were entwined back and forth with America. Martin's grandfather could not read or write, and his

Martin Naughton in Stackallan.

Martin, Carmel, their son Neil and his wife Deirdre, outside the family home.

wife, Mary Nally, was brought back from New York in a made 'match' in order to join the Naughton and the Nally farms together. She was a bright, smart woman, who could certainly read and write. When she died, she left the Naughton land to her children, but returned the Nally farm to her own family. (In 2007, Martin's wife Carmel bought back the Naughton home farm at Belcarra as a birthday present for Martin; the old homestead has now been rebuilt). As a child, Martin's mother was sent out to an aunt in New Haven in Connecticut and spent her formative years there. She returned to Ireland on holiday where she met her future husband.

Because the farm could only sustain one son, Martin Naughton Sr. had to leave his beloved Mayo; he walked all the way to Castlebar to enlist in the Gardaí Síochana (the Irish police). He eventually became a highly respected Garda (policeman) in Dundalk, County Louth, where he was regarded as strong, strict and utterly fair. There were seven children in the family, two boys and five girls. All the family remained in Ireland, which was exceptional for large Irish families of that generation. Their mother was very devout, and Martin's elder brother Richard is currently parish priest of Cloghogue near Newry.

The Naughton parents instilled traditional values in their children, prioritising education and emphasising the total sacrifice that was necessary to educate the family. Their bedrock virtues stressed unwavering commitment to what was best for the family as a whole. Martin attended the De La Salle primary and secondary schools in Dundalk during World War II. Of the one hundred boys who started, only eleven completed the Intermediate Certificate (Junior High) and a mere nine obtained the Leaving Certificate (High School). 91% of his fellow students did not get a Leaving Certificate, and 80% had left formal education before they were fourteen.

After Secondary School, the only 'good' jobs available in Ireland were the Civil Service, teaching, and the army; none appealed to the young Martin Naughton. In 1956, the sixteen-year old boy took the boat to Southampton in England. His mother was so distressed that her son was forced to go to 'pagan' England that she vowed that she would never vote in Ireland again. When Martin arrived in England, he had an annoying pain in his shoulder. He discovered that his mother had sewn many miraculous medals into the lining of his coat.

Martin Naughton paid his own way through college for five years, working in the evenings and at weekends to finance his education – casual labour in bakeries, all kinds of jobs. He returned home twice a year, in the summer and at Christmas. The teenager, isolated from his family, took it on the chin: 'it will take five years to do this and I am just going to tough it out'. When he got homesick, he would go down to Goodwood Clatford, a train station near Andover, to gaze at a Paul Henry poster advertising holidays in the West of Ireland. He bought a painting just like it when he saw it in a window in London, long before he could afford it – it cost a whole week's wages to pay for it. He carried that painting of Connemara around with him through various 'digs' and flats. It was the first serious painting that Martin, later a renowned art collector, ever bought. He still owns it.

Martin studied aeronautical engineering because he was advised that it was a career for the future, and there was a vibrant aeronautical tradition around Southampton. While still at college, he obtained a coveted work placement on release periods with Hawker Siddeley, a renowned military aircraft manufacturer, who had cutting-edge engineering standards. When the British Government announced that they were cutting back on military spending in 1959, he switched to mechanical and production engineering, which became a growing passion. He graduated in 1961, aged twenty-one.

In Shannon County Clare, he joined an American electronics company called SPS, who were based in Jenkintown, Pennsylvania. In those days, there were incentives to locate at Shannon. It was the first duty-free airport in the world and you could bring your materials in duty-free, manufacture, and ship out. It was a state within a state: you had to pass through customs and emigration to enter the work zone at Shannon. It was based on Irish labour, but the management was all American, German and British.

Shannon, a new town, comprised entirely of young people, was a lively place to live and work. The young folk went out together and made their own fun, holding lively céilis (musical get-togethers) in the various pubs and houses. Martin loved Irish traditional music and Clare was the home of it. He knew where to find the music and the craic (enjoyment), and he followed that scene around, making weekend forays into West Clare or down to Kerry. At that time, pre-television, people were more adept at making their own fun. When the first television aerial was being erected, everyone agreed that it would ruin Shannon and the advent of TV certainly changed people's patterns of socialising.

Highly trained at Southampton, Martin found himself in the right place at the right time and he was already a manager at twenty-one years of age. Six months later, he was offered a job at GEC in Dunleer, County Louth, a big electrical appliance manufacturer that made products behind the tariff barrier with guaranteed quotas that protected fledgling Irish industry. His immediate boss at Shannon had moved to GEC: they asked him if he knew anyone who could manage the industrial engineering department, which had a dozen engineers and a big backup staff. Knowing that Martin was from County Louth, he asked him if he would be interested. Martin went for an interview and the boss there said 'this job pays £1500 a year, but I couldn't give you £1500 a year, it would ruin you. Would you do it for a thousand?' Martin agreed and got a company car and all the trimmings. A decade later, he was the plant manager.

He had been briefly headhunted to another American company down in Shannon and was headhunted back again. After Seán Lemass stepped down as Taoiseach in 1966, he joined the board of GEC. Martin's old friend of the thousand pounds tried to recruit him back. He declined because he had just got engaged and his fiancé Carmel McCarthy was teaching close by in Limerick; they had bought a site at Shannon, they were building a house, and they intended to put down roots there. He was then invited to have dinner with Lemass, who Martin admired as the architect of Ireland's economic transformation. At that dinner, the politician proved sufficiently persuasive to inspire Martin to return to prepare the company for entry to the European Economic Community [EEC]. He ended up running the plant. Martin and Carmel were married in 1968 and three children soon formed a lively family.

GEC was in difficulty, with the Irish accession to the EEC in 1973 looming. Martin formulated a new direction, as he saw no future in the way that GEC was operating. His plan was rejected. Martin decided that if what he was proposing was the correct policy, then he should act on his convictions. He set up his own business to implement that plan. With four colleagues, he started Glen Electric in 1973, employing seven people in Newry just across the border in Northern Ireland. The plan was to grow to one hundred employees and never to get any bigger than that. As young entrepreneurs, it was hugely exciting to talk about starting your own business over pints or coffee. In the cold light of a Dunleer morning, relinquishing the steady job and the reassuring salary was an entirely different matter. The newly married Naughtons had three young children, and it was risky to start all over again. Carmel was very much involved, highly supportive, and completely committed as a risk-taker. Only the innocence and optimism of youth carried them over the line, as they were supremely confident that they could pull this off. They knew the business inside out and they had decided to concentrate on electric heating.

Of that period, Martin comments:

> When you start your own business, you really have no idea what it takes, because no matter how hard you work for somebody else, a different dimension emerges when you work for yourself. It requires twenty-four hours a day utter commitment, and the sole alternative is going bust. You have to be driven.

Every hour he could work, Martin was working. He worked seven days a week. He worked until he got so tired that he could not work anymore: he grabbed a few hours sleep, and then worked again. He lost the habit of having time off – he worked nights, he worked weekends, he worked holidays. He accepted that this was just what he had to do to succeed. When they worked late on dismal winter nights or on sunny Sunday afternoons, they would encourage each other: 'Our competitors are out now gallivanting, sinking pints or putts'.

Meanwhile, Carmel provided the necessary ballast and security at home. Born in Monaghan and educated at St. Louis Convent and Mary Immaculate Teacher Training College, Carmel's first career was as a schoolteacher. She would later continue her own education by taking the Diploma in European Painting at Trinity College, and by studying Japanese there.

Four years after its founding, in an astonishing move, the fledgling Irish company Glen bought the then brand leaders, Dimplex, who were based in Southampton. Martin's was the first Irish company to buy an English company and it detonated shockwaves throughout the industry. Today any Irish company could buy any company anywhere in the

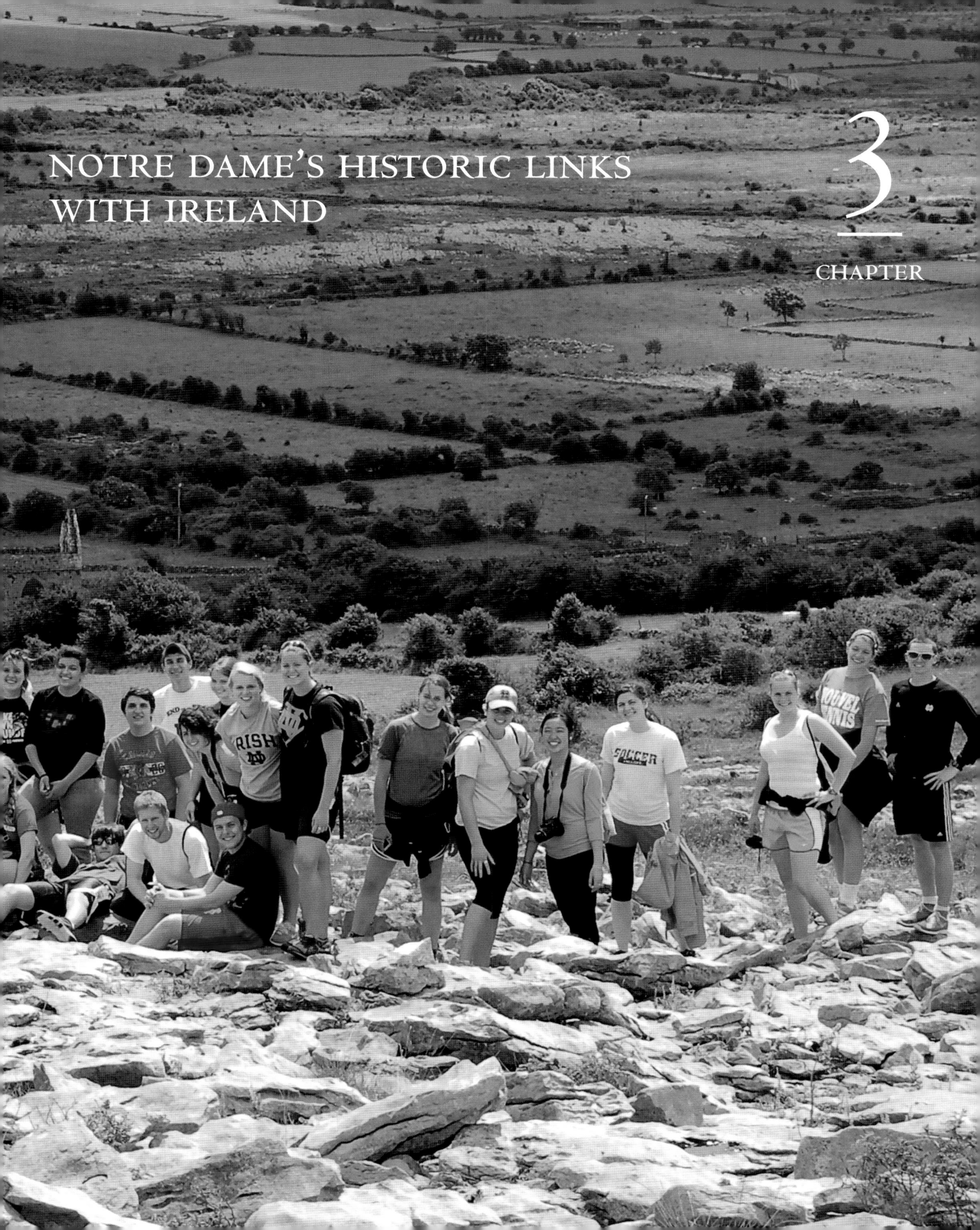

CHAPTER 3

NOTRE DAME'S HISTORIC LINKS WITH IRELAND

NOTRE DAME'S HISTORIC LINKS WITH IRELAND

Notre Dame was founded in 1842 and since then, fifteen of its seventeen Presidents have been of Irish-descent. Of the Congregation of Holy Cross (CSC) brothers who accompanied Father Sorin on the expedition to South Bend, only two were French. The others were Irish: Peter and Patrick (both farmers), Basil (a cooper), and William (a carpenter). Their practical skills were pivotal to establishing a viable physical presence on the wintry plains of Northern Indiana. The same was true of Irish women: in 1843, four CSC sisters came from France to assist the fledgling college; their first recruit was the twenty-year old Bridget Coffey from Ireland. In 1849, the first two ND graduates were Richard Shortis from Cork and Neal Gillespie, an Irish-American. From the get go, Irish men and women were in at the ground floor of building Notre Dame as a great Irish-American institution.

For example, on the same steamer bringing the young Andrew Morrissey, a future President of the University, to America, there was also a teenage Irish girl who intended to enter the convent at ND. Sister Martha became the head of the busy ND kitchen from 1900 to 1923. Students remembered her as the 'Sister of the silver finger'. In filleting fish one day, a bone pierced her finger, and she nearly lost it. The bone was replaced with a small rod of silver, and it was with this finger that she directed the hungry students. For twenty-three years, she laboured in the kitchen, until her death on 4 April 1923 – a silver sister under the golden dome. While we remember the inspiring leaders, we should also recall Sister Martha, and the many other humble Irish men and women who served Notre Dame loyally in lives dedicated to the development and functioning of a great university.

Ironically, Fr. Sorin himself only tolerated the Irish if they were subservient and submissive. An Irishman who dared to differ with him was condemned on account of his nationality, because the austere Frenchman thought that the volatile Irish temper was incompatible with strict religious obedience. Sorin defended a harassed bishop on the grounds that the accusing priests were 'all of them Irish'. Sorin's clerical formation was in the rigorist tradition of the French church emerging out of the shadow of the French Revolution, which placed a high premium on orthodoxy and unquestioning obedience to constituted authority, whereas the Irish church of the O'Connellite period was combative, democratic and well versed in tackling entrenched authority.

PRESIDENTS OF NOTRE DAME

Edward Sorin (1842–1865)
Patrick Dillon (1865–1866)
William Corby (1866–1872; 1877–1881)
Auguste Lemonnier (1872–1874)
Patrick Colovin (1875–1877)
Thomas Walsh (1881–1893)
Andrew Morrissey (1893–1905)
John W. Cavanaugh (1905–1919)
James Burns (1919—1922)
Matthew Walsh (1922–1928)
Charles O'Donnell (1928–1934)
John O'Hara (1934–1940)
J. Hugh O'Donnell (1940–1946)
John J. Cavanaugh (1946–1952)
Theodore Hesburgh (1952–1987)
Edward 'Monk' Malloy (1987–2005)
John Jenkins (2005–)

The resulting culture clash could have its amusing side. In the early days, a small balcony ran around the edge of the dome, and although the access door was kept locked, resourceful students occasionally got through. Tim O'Sullivan infiltrated it at dawn on 17 March 1867 and trumpeted 'St. Patrick's Day in the Morning' over the sleepy campus. Sorin explicitly prohibited any special celebration of St. Patrick's Day, especially the 'Wearing of the Green'. Two novices, Dave O'Leary and John Quinn, were so incensed that they extracted the green ribbon from the missal in the chapel, cut it in two, pinned it on their surplices, and marched into the sanctuary. Sorin impulsively expelled them.

As late as 1877, the battle was still being fought over whether ND should celebrate St. Patrick's Day, even though most of its students were of Irish extraction. Some still felt that ND ought to be a place 'of dry study merely' but others argued that 'according to a custom of long standing ... entertainments are always given the evening before, and as the day following is a holiday, the extra sleep in no way interferes with their studies'. An early 'census' of student ethnicities in 1872 found that 421 students self-described as follows: 183 of Irish extraction; 155 Americans; 75 German; 21 French; 3 Spanish; 2 Scotch; 1 English and 1 Italian.

THE ORIGINS OF THE 'FIGHTING IRISH'

The Irish found the perfect opportunity to demonstrate their American loyalty in the Civil War between 1861-1865. If they were willing to risk their lives by fighting for the United States of America, then it would be virtually impossible to question their loyalty. The Irish were heavily involved in the Civil War, more often as members of the Union Army, unsurprisingly as more Irish settled in the North. Thirty-eight Union regiments had the word 'Irish' in their names, and at least 170,000 Irish-born men served in the Union Army. The most famous of these regiments was New York's 'Fighting 69th' – the original 'Fighting Irish' – which lost 196 of its 317 men at Antietam and 128 of 238 men at Fredericksburg. As these death tolls suggest, the Irish were courageous soldiers, known for their unflinching valour and willingness to lay down their lives for the Union cause. The fact that the Irish spilled their blood serving their adopted country was the strongest proof possible that they were not half-hearted patriots, hyphenated Americans whose real allegiance lay with another country.

When the Irish regiments formed in the American Civil War, they immediately looked back to the proud expatriate Irish military tradition for inspiration. The original Irish Brigades had fought with the Catholic armies of continental Europe in the seventeenth and eighteenth centuries. These Irish Brigades bled significant numbers at the Battles of Fontenoy (1745) and Laffeldt (1747), where they established their credentials as shock troops. Their war cry, derived from the Irish language, was Fág an Bealach (Clear the Way), and the Brigades attracted an enormous reputation for the 'Fighting Irish', when the Catholics of Ireland had no army of their own to join.

When the American Civil War began, the 69th New York was the most renowned of the regiments, constituting the 'Irish Brigade' of the First Division, Second Corps, Army of the Potomac. They self-consciously modelled themselves on the expatriate Irish Brigades of the eighteenth century, assuming their motto 'Fág an Bealach' and calling themselves the 'Fighting Irish'. Like the eighteenth-century Irish Brigades, they envisaged themselves as an Irish Army in exile, who would learn military skills and then return to free Ireland from British rule. They were heavily recruited from the Famine immigrants to New York, who had turned that place into the most Irish city in the world by 1860 – more than one quarter of a million Irish-born people lived there.

Catholic chaplains of the Irish Brigade, in the Union army at Harrison's Landing, Virginia, 1862. Seated, left to right: Captain J. J. McCormack, James Dillon, CSC, and William Corby, CSC. Standing: Patrick Dillon, CSC, and Dr. K. O'Hanlon.

During the American Civil War, no less than seven Notre Dame priests served as chaplains: Peter Cooney, Paul Gillen, James Dillon (all Irish), William Corby (Irish-American), Julian Bourget, Zepherin Lévêque and Joseph Carrier. Fathers Dillon, Gillen and Corby were chaplains to the celebrated Irish Brigade. Corby notes proudly that the rattled Confederates would shout 'Here comes that damned green flag again', whenever the Irish Brigade appeared. On 1 June 1862, at the Battle of Fair Oaks, Corby recorded how 'they advanced with their well-known war-shout [Fág an Bealach], and closed with fearful ferocity on the foe, and for an hour mowed them down almost by companies'. At Antietam on 17 September 1862, the Irish Brigade was once more first in the fray. At the moment when the 'double-quick' order was issued, Fr. Corby was at the rear.

> I gave rein to my horse, and let him go at full gallop till I reached the front of the Brigade, and, passing along the line, told the men to make an act of contrition. As they were coming toward me on the double-quick, I had time only to wheel my horse for an instant toward them and gave my poor men a hasty absolution, and rode on with General [Thomas Francis] Meagher into the battle ... In twenty or thirty minutes after this absolution, 506 of these very men lay on the field, either dead or wounded ... I shall never forget how wicked the whiz of the enemy's bullets seemed as we advanced into that battle. As soon as my men began to fall, I dismounted and began to hear their confessions on the spot. Every instant bullets whizzed past my head ... the bullets came from the Confederates at very close range.

At Gettysburg in 1863, Corby approached Colonel Patrick Kelly, imploring: 'For two or three weeks, we have been marching constantly. My men have not had a chance to get to confession. I must give them one last bit of spiritual comfort. Let me stand up on this rock, where they may all see me. Let me speak to them'. Corby instructed the soldiers that he was offering a general absolution, because individual confessions were impossible.

A marvellous letter in the Hesburgh Library archives offers support to the accuracy of Fr. Corby's description of the Irish Brigade. Thomas Francis McGrath (1839–1922), an immigrant from County Kilkenny, served in the 69th New York Infantry from 1861 to 1865, rising to the rank of first lieutenant. He fought in many of the Eastern theatre's major actions. Wounded at Gettysburg and again at Spotsylvania, he was captured before Petersburg. Writing from a hospital in Chester County, Pennsylvania in 1863, his characteristically Irish letter (see opposite page) began by assuring his mother that her son was in good health, before getting to the gory details.

The Notre Dame's chaplains association with the Irish Brigade, especially Fr. Corby's iconic role in some of the most important battles, created an indelible link between ND and the 'Fighting Irish'. Only three Brigade flags survive from the period: one was donated to Notre Dame by Colonel James Brady, who served with Fr. Corby – it now resides in the Snite Gallery; a second is in the regimental HQ in New York; a third was given to the Irish people by President John

The Band of the Fighting Irish spells out Notre Dame's heritage.

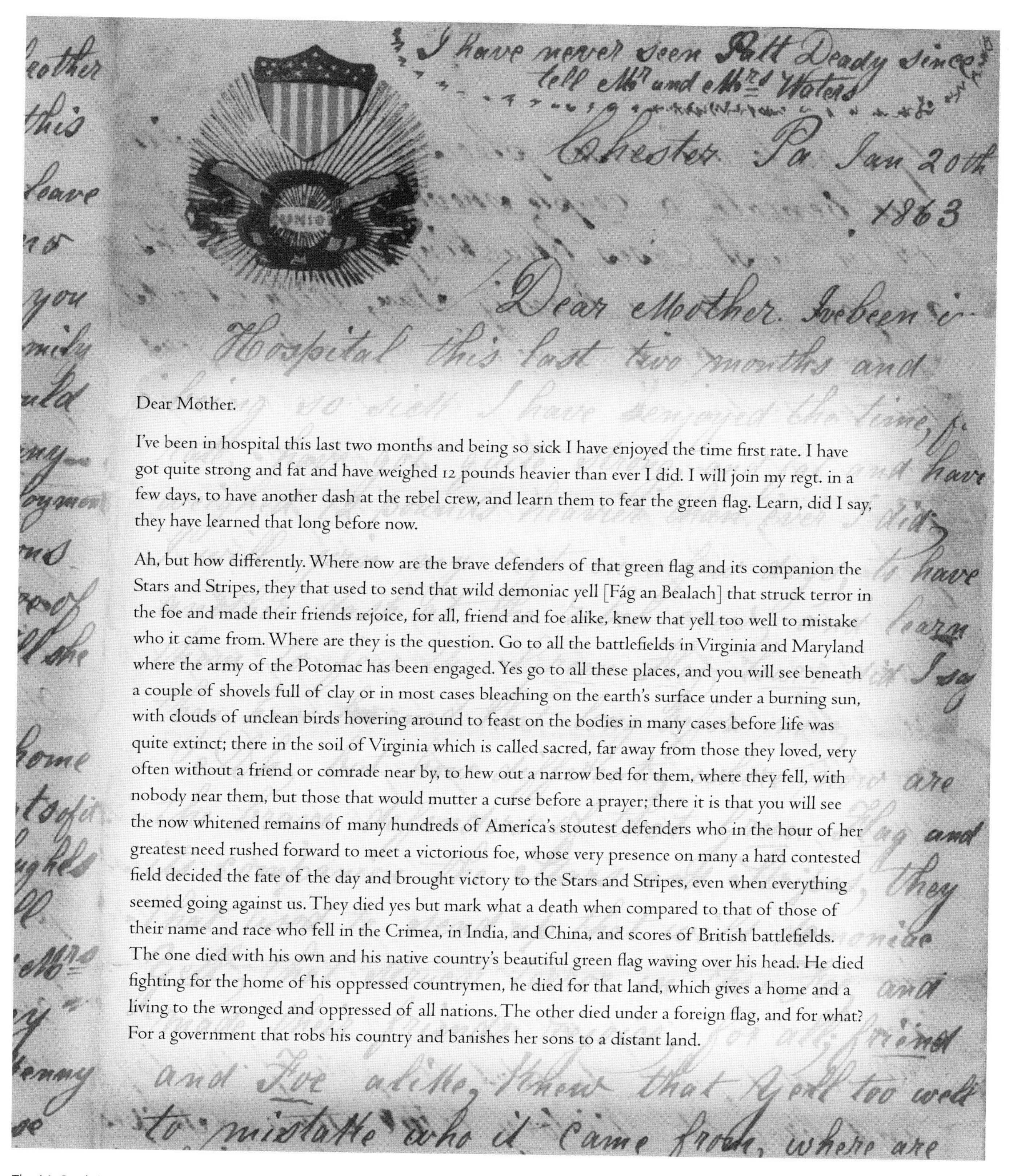

Dear Mother.

I've been in hospital this last two months and being so sick I have enjoyed the time first rate. I have got quite strong and fat and have weighed 12 pounds heavier than ever I did. I will join my regt. in a few days, to have another dash at the rebel crew, and learn them to fear the green flag. Learn, did I say, they have learned that long before now.

Ah, but how differently. Where now are the brave defenders of that green flag and its companion the Stars and Stripes, they that used to send that wild demoniac yell [Fág an Bealach] that struck terror in the foe and made their friends rejoice, for all, friend and foe alike, knew that yell too well to mistake who it came from. Where are they is the question. Go to all the battlefields in Virginia and Maryland where the army of the Potomac has been engaged. Yes go to all these places, and you will see beneath a couple of shovels full of clay or in most cases bleaching on the earth's surface under a burning sun, with clouds of unclean birds hovering around to feast on the bodies in many cases before life was quite extinct; there in the soil of Virginia which is called sacred, far away from those they loved, very often without a friend or comrade near by, to hew out a narrow bed for them, where they fell, with nobody near them, but those that would mutter a curse before a prayer; there it is that you will see the now whitened remains of many hundreds of America's stoutest defenders who in the hour of her greatest need rushed forward to meet a victorious foe, whose very presence on many a hard contested field decided the fate of the day and brought victory to the Stars and Stripes, even when everything seemed going against us. They died yes but mark what a death when compared to that of those of their name and race who fell in the Crimea, in India, and China, and scores of British battlefields. The one died with his own and his native country's beautiful green flag waving over his head. He died fighting for the home of his oppressed countrymen, he died for that land, which gives a home and a living to the wronged and oppressed of all nations. The other died under a foreign flag, and for what? For a government that robs his country and banishes her sons to a distant land.

The McGrath Letter 1863, from Hesburgh Library, Notre Dame.

Senator Mark Daly stands in front of the Irish Brigade Flag in Dáil Éireann, with a group of ND students, Spring 2012.

Fitzgerald Kennedy during his poignant visit in 1963. The President was massively popular in Ireland as the first Irish-American Catholic to occupy the White House, and his gift was intensely symbolic, as he himself acknowledged in his presentation speech:

> In the fall of 1862, after serving with distinction and gallantry in some of the toughest fighting of this most bloody struggle, the Irish Brigade was presented with a new set of flags. In the city ceremony, the city chamberlain gave them the motto, 'The Union, Our Country, and Ireland forever'. Their old ones having been torn to shreds in previous battles, Capt. Richard McGee took possession of these flags on December Second in New York City and arrived with them at the Battle of Fredericksburg and carried them in the battle. Today, in recognition of what these gallant Irishmen and what millions of other Irish have done for my country, and through the generosity of the 'Fighting 69th', I would like to present one of these flags to the people of Ireland.

From the Heart: Patrick Griffin, Madden-Hennebry Professor of Irish-American History

Notre Dame is a wonderful place to teach Irish-American history. The topic fascinates students, many of whom take great pride in their Irish heritage. The place also stands as a living monument to the rags-to-riches narrative that animates much of Irish-American identity. For many Irish-Americans, the nickname the 'Fighting Irish' epitomises the mythic story that many believe defines the group. Once a term of derision, 'fighting Irish' now resonates as a point of pride.

Notre Dame also holds surprises. When I was preparing a lecture on Éamon De Valera's visit to the university during his 1919 American tour, I discovered that on the stop he viewed and held the Civil War sword of Thomas Francis Meagher. Known as a leader of the failed Young Irelander rising of 1848, Meagher championed a republican tradition that sought to free Ireland by any means necessary. For his efforts, 'Meagher of the Sword'(as he is remembered in Ireland) escaped the hangman's noose only to be exiled in Van Diemen's Land. Eventually, he was smuggled on board ship, reaching San Francisco to a tumultuous welcome, before making his way to New York. Here, in the wake of Bull Run, he would found the famous Irish Brigade.

Meagher saw no contradiction in fighting for the stars and stripes and fighting for Ireland. He believed, as did Famine immigrants, that the cause of American freedom was Ireland's as well. Meagher believed that the true republican was home in both nations. After the war, General Meagher became first territorial governor of Montana, a place awash with Irish immigrants. Senator Thomas Walsh of Montana presented the sword to the university in 1914.

So when De Valera touched that sword at Notre Dame, a little more than fifty years after Meagher had brandished it in battle, he was gesturing toward what he regarded as a vital relationship between Irish and American freedom, one that the American-born De Valera epitomised. When he visited places like Notre Dame, he was travelling as President of the Irish Republic fighting for its freedom. But he was also journeying through his homeland, a different country, to be sure, but one that Irishmen and women had fought for. In many ways, as he was touring the country to raise funds and increase the visibility of the Irish cause for independence, he came looking for America to repay a debt for freedom that the United States owed to Ireland. Americans were happy to pay, none more so than the jubilant students at Notre Dame. So moved was he by his time at Notre Dame that De Valera considered it the highpoint of his American tour. Although no one knows for sure the exact origins of the nickname 'the Fighting Irish', it is little coincidence that the term gained general currency in the 1919 football season in the wake of De Valera's visit. He was, after all, the most celebrated fighting Irishman in America at the time.

I was astonished to learn that Notre Dame had the sword of 'Meagher of the Sword'. But I could not find it. Eventually I did. It lay stored in a grey box in the sixth floor of the library's archives. Archivists were not to be blamed; rather, it seemed the significance of the sword had somehow gone missing. Notre Dame, after all, was more Irish-American, with an emphasis on American, than Irish by the turn of the twenty-first century.

I found more. Notre Dame also owned a flag of the famed Irish Brigade. Like the sword, the flag was nowhere to be found. I later discovered that it had been exhibited from time to time but was held for the moment in an off-campus storage facility. The flag, referred to as the Second Colors, was made by Tiffany and Co. in 1862 and presented to Meagher by the grateful citizens of New York. On it is emblazoned the name of one of the regiments of the Irish Brigade: the New York 63rd. Along with the famed 69th, the Brigade comprised New York's 88th, as well as regiments from Pennsylvania and Massachusetts. By the time the 'Second Colors' were commissioned, the first had been shredded but never surrendered in some of the bloodiest fighting of the Civil War.

The Irish Brigade had distinguished itself in the Peninsula Campaign, and the green flag came to be feared by rebels. Meagher's men earned the reputation as the shock troops of the Army of the Potomac, leading Abraham Lincoln to visit Meagher's camp and enticing him to kiss the colors. The Brigade went on to win fame and court death at Antietam

This flag of the Fourth Massachusetts Regiment of the Irish Brigade bears the slogan Fág an Bealach (Clear the Way) along its left-hand margin.

and Fredericksburg. Here, on one afternoon it lost 1,200 of 2,000 men. By the time the Brigade fought on the second day at Gettysburg in the Wheatfield, it was a shell of itself.

The flag of the 63rd was to be used for ceremonial purposes, when the remnants of the brigade marched in Washington and New York following the North's victory in the War. Father William Corby, Holy Cross priest, chaplain to the Irish Brigade, and eventually President of Notre Dame, secured the flag for the university. He hoped that all the flags of the Brigade would find a home at Notre Dame because of its connection to the Brigade, its central location, and its growing stature within Irish America. De Valera viewed this flag as he toured Notre Dame.

Like the sword, the flag also speaks to the real and durable connections between Ireland and America. In June 1963, when John F. Kennedy made his triumphal tour of Ireland – where he was first welcomed by President De Valera – he formally addressed the Dáil in Leinster House. Here, he presented the Irish Parliament with the second 'Tiffany Colors' of the Fighting 69th. An exact replica of Notre Dame's flag, the colours Kennedy presented adorn the walls of Leinster House to this day. Kennedy gave the flag to the Irish in grateful recognition for all they had done for the cause of American freedom, a history that Kennedy was eager to recount. He knew that one-third of the Continental Army under Washington was Irish, leading a British commander to lament 'we have lost America through the Irish'. He also knew of the exploits of the Irish Brigade. In his address to the Dáil, he regaled TDs with the role that Meagher had played in American history. The bonds that both the flag and sword represented were not lost on Kennedy. The great-grandson of eight famine immigrants, Kennedy joked that if Ireland had not had to fight for its freedom, he might be sitting with his audience in the Dáil, and if De Valera had never left New York, he – not Kennedy – might be addressing the Dáil as a president of the United States.

Like De Valera a generation earlier, Kennedy had travelled the ocean as a self-proclaimed apostle of liberty. The 'Fighting Irish' flag suggested the continuing significance of the bonds between Ireland and America. It also speaks to the continuing and evolving significance of Ireland in the American story and of America in the Irish story, the sacrifices of ordinary men and women, and the viability of Irish-American history at places like Notre Dame.

WHY 'FIGHTING IRISH'? A SECOND STRAND

If the close links to the Fighting 69th and Fr. Corby offer one route as to why Notre Dame became known as the 'Fighting Irish', a second strand is the anti-Irish and anti-Catholic prejudice which disfigured American life in the nineteenth and early twentieth centuries. America featured a long parade of witch burners and anti-Papist Know Nothings (aka the American Party, founded in 1854), The Ku Klux Klan, and prohibitionists. *The Awful Disclosures of the Hotel Dieu Nunnery* was the biggest best seller in America until *Uncle Tom's Cabin*. The historian Richard Hofstadter famously described anti-Catholicism as the pornography of the Puritan. In the White Slave panic of 1910, one newspaper asked: 'Shall we defend our American civilisation or lower our flag to the most despicable foreigners – French, Irish, Italians, Jews and Mongolians?' The Irish in America often found themselves at the uncomfortable vortex of the confluence of anti-Catholicism, evangelicalism, and scientific racism.

When the KKK revived in 1915, it did so as an anti-immigration force, concentrating on the threat posed to true blue 100% Americans. Klan parades, in full regalia, were very much in vogue and one was planned for South Bend on 17 May 1924. The burly football-playing students of Notre Dame defended immigrant Catholic communities in South Bend. This caused an outraged 'kluxer' to protest to President Walsh of Notre Dame about his 'bunch of Mackerel Snapping Anarchists from Notre Dame':

> You can thank your lucky stars that you have your buildings intack, for if the Knights of the Ku Klux Klan assembled in South Bend last Sat. had been as lawless as your bunch of Anarchist students they would have wiped the Notre Dame buildings off the earth.
>
> The klansman is taught to respect the law, which is more than the Rufneck Anarchists attending your school are taught, judging from their lawless acts last Saturday. For no cause at all the car I was riding in on my way peacefully through the city of South Bend last Sat. was suddenly attacked by your bunch of Anarchist Ruffains and the car damaged, and we escaped bodily injury by putting on speed and rushing through the traffic. Things have come to a pretty pass when an American citizen cannot ride peacefully through the streets of an American city without being set upon by a band of hoodlums and ruffains.
>
> You had better spend some time in your classes in teaching patriotism and respect for the American Flag. Time and again your bunch of Anarchists tore the American flag to bits.
>
> I have heard the Knights of Columbus deny that they took such an oath as has been circulated among the public, but after reading in history of the bloody murders during the French Revolution, and knowing of conditions as they exist today under Catholic dominition in South America, and seeing with my own eyes some of the things that the bunch of Mackerel Snapping Anarchists from Notre Dame did last Saturday, I can easily believe that every word in the K of C oath is true.
>
> You will see that the Klan will grow by leaps and bounds in and around South Bend. Your hoodlums couldn't have done anything to help along the cause of the Klan any better, for some of the American public will be awakened to the great need of the hour.
>
> We showed you a few tricks at the recent Primary, now we are going to show you several more at the election in the Fall.
>
> I say down with Catholic dominition of every kind in AMARICA,
>
> Sincerely, A KLUXER,

In 1927, when the Catholic Al Smith stood in the presidential election, he was undermined by scurrilous raw sectarianism. It is against this backdrop that we can understand more clearly why Notre Dame reacted by challenging a negative stereotype and turning it into a positive. Fr. Charles Carey, CSC, penned an illuminating little essay in 1953 called 'Why the 'Fighting Irish?':

> Many people wonder (or worry) about Notre Dame and that word, Irish. To us, it doesn't mean race exclusively; nor is it just another nickname. The fact is, it keeps alive the memory of a long, uphill fight for recognition against a spirit that was not always generous, nor even fair-minded. The Irish, as known at Notre Dame, has an authentic history and a meaning deeper even than race. Notre Dame began athletic relations chiefly with local colleges founded by various denominations. Press reports would refer to the schools as the 'Baptists' or the 'Methodists', and the like. For Notre Dame it was the 'Catholics', or the 'Irish'. But the players were never all of Irish ancestry; nor were they all Catholics. The usage was not original, but a continuing

> custom from earlier Colonial times. The bulk of the first Catholic immigrants were Irish – so that Catholics and Irish were identical in the public mind. It is sad to recall now, but few of the original states were without laws against them. Advertisements for 'Help Wanted' commonly carried the restriction: 'No Catholics. No Irish'. The Puritans were the first to cry: 'Stop the Irish!' When the religious origin of other colleges lost its significance, the emphasis shifted to conventional names, and to their school colors.
>
> But history is recorded remembrance in our blessed heritage here at Notre Dame. Fighting Irish! It's more than a name; more than a people. It is the Faith! In narrow, little New England, it began as a slur – a term of opprobrium. But we took it up and made of it a badge of honor – a symbol of fidelity and courage to everyone who suffers from discrimination; to everyone who has an uphill fight for the elemental decencies, and the basic Christian principles woven into the texture of our nation. Preserving this tradition, and this meaning of Irish at Notre Dame, does honor to every one of us. It explains why Lewinski belongs here; why Alessandrini is the Irish leader; why Schmaltz belongs here; why Bertrand, and Moreau, Van Dyke, and Larson feel at home here as much as do Leahy and O'Brien.

It is against this nativist backdrop that the term 'Fighting Irish' stands out clearly as the positive reversal of a stereotype rather than as an act of aggression or ethnic tribalism. As current president Fr. John Jenkins, CSC, notes, the 'Fighting Irish' nickname began as a slur by opponents 'but the university embraced that name and transformed it to represent the real resilience of the Irish'.

In the 1920s, Notre Dame sports teams were first widely nicknamed the 'Fighting Irish' – Knute Rockne famously said of his multi-ethnic team 'they are all Irish to me' – and they gained national followings from Irish-Americans and others as Catholics entered the American mainstream. Notre Dame, the feisty outsiders from the Midwest, took it to the then dominant Ivy Leagues, crushing Princeton 25-2 in 1923, and winning College Football national championships in 1924, 1929 and 1930. In a smart move, free national radio broadcasts (revenue losers but big brand builders) generated a loyal 'subway alum' base across the Irish-American Catholic community. Fr. Arthur Hope, CSC, recalls the 'thousands of rosaries and innumerable prayers offered by cloistered nuns on the Saturdays of Autumn – by women who hardly know the difference between a touch-down and a clipping penalty'. To this day, Notre Dame, unique among College Football teams, has all its games broadcast nationally on radio and television.

Among Notre Dame's staunchest supporters was the celebrated Irish tenor Count John McCormack. He received the Laetare medal in 1933 from Fr. O'Donnell, who observed: 'You have made Ireland's voice audible to millions who have never seen Ireland's face'. McCormack popularised the 'Notre Dame Night' broadcast in the early days of radio, introducing it on NBC's Red Network.

This valuable national profile allowed the university to set higher ambitions for itself. Fr. Andrew Morrissey, CSC, born at Thomastown, County Kilkenny, and ND president from 1893 to 1905, had argued: 'What we need here is a compact, tidy little boarding school. We can't compete with these other institutions that have all the money. Our very existence depends on giving Catholic boys a good preparatory foundation'. He was opposed by the more scholarly but stand-offish Fr. John Zahm, CSC, the first distinguished scientist on campus, who believed that Notre Dame should aspire to be a proper university rather than a glorified boarding school. Success on the football team was parlayed into increasing national prestige and visibility, which in turn attracted resources and allowed Notre Dame to develop into a more ambitious university.

The historical context of the 'Fighting Irish' still infuses Notre Dame's football programme. A painting called 'The Original Fighting Irish' (by former ND lacrosse player Revere La Noue) is highly visible in the office of Notre Dame football coach Brian Kelly's office. Kelly commented: 'You see blue-collar. You see a bit of swagger. You see toughness. Growing up as an Irish Catholic in Boston, that's what I remember Notre Dame being. That's been one of our goals every day – to get that fight back in the Fighting Irish. It's good because that's who I am'.

THE ORIGINS OF FOOTBALL AT NOTRE DAME: SOCCER, RUGBY, GAELIC FOOTBALL OR AMERICAN FOOTBALL?

There is one little-known Irish element in the story of Notre Dame football. Reports of early games on campus make it abundantly clear that whatever game was played, it was not American football as we know it now. Informal football games started at Notre Dame in the late 1860s. They were organised by the students and tolerated by the University unless its roughness got out of hand: as the *Scholastic* noted in 1870, 'We hope the good old game of football will soon be the fashion'. Frequently, a keg of cider or a barrel of apples was the prize for the Reds and the Blues, as the two teams were usually called.

These early games bear a tantalising similarity to reports of Irish football games at the same time – a mix of soccer, rugby and wrestling, where brute force was more important than skill, and huge teams were the order of the day. In 1876, for example, 'one of the old fashioned games of football' was played on campus on a Fall day. Ben Heeb of Dubuque and Jim Hagerty of St. Louis chose sides, not 'on account of their age or size, as they were both rather young', but because 'they could play more football for their inches than any other boys in the place'. There were forty-two boys on each team. The phases of play were called 'innings', lasting until the ball had been borne across the goal. Each side scored two goals and the fourth 'inning' took forty-five minutes of pushing and tussling, when the umpire decided to call the game.

Almost every feature of this game could be replicated in reports of football games of the same period in Ireland. The same holds true for another game played in 1879: 'The Reds scored the winning goal after one hour and forty minutes to triumph two-one'. In 1881, in a further red/blue encounter, 120 students played. With the scores tied at one goal each, 'all were so thoroughly exhausted that they were willing to call it a tie'.

Whatever these games were (a hybrid of soccer, rugby and Gaelic football?), they were hardly American football. An even more telling piece of evidence attends the first official Notre Dame intercollegiate football game played against the University of Michigan on 23 November 1887. Michigan, the champion team of the West, left Ann Arbor to play a series of games in the Northwest. Michigan stopped off on its way through South Bend to play a picked team of the senior department. However Michigan played according to the rules of rugby, which were not understood at ND. Notre Dame still agreed to play the champions according to rugby rules, if Michigan first explained them. A meeting was then held to organise a rugby football association under the presidency of athletics director Brother Paul and new uniforms were ordered. 'The jacket and trousers are of canvas, the stockings are brown and black by which colors the teams will be distinguished'. This evidence establishes quite clearly that this first official Notre Dame football game was really a game of rugby. Perhaps it is appropriate that Notre Dame play Navy in the Aviva Stadium in 2012, home of the Irish rugby team!

A portrait of William Butler Yeats which hangs in the Keough Naughton Centre.

WILLIAM BUTLER YEATS AT NOTRE DAME 1904 AND 1933

Once Notre Dame was firmly established on the national educational stage, and once its Irish identity was widely known across the nation, it began to feature more prominently in Irish cultural circles. Proof of that enhanced visibility and prestige was the fact that William Butler Yeats spent several days at Notre Dame in mid January 1904. The New York based Irish-American lawyer John Quinn organised the visit and praised the university: 'Notre Dame is more generous than any other Catholic College in taking two lectures'. By contrast, Quinn was incensed at the University of Chicago, which tried to lower the poet's fees and still charged for admission – behaviour that Yeats deemed 'shabby'. En route to South Bend from Chicago, he spoke to the engineering students at Purdue, where the going was tough – the students were like 'wet sand' – before speaking at Washington Hall on 'Poetry' on 15 January. The next day, he gave four lectures – two at Saint Mary's, and two at ND – followed by a class in the afternoon of the 16th on 'Poetry, Sligo, Innisfree and Thoreau' and a lecture that night on 'The Intellectual Revival'.

Despite his packed schedule, Yeats enjoyed himself: 'I like the priests here very much – huge men full of vitality. I am in the best of spirits and health'. Yeats opined that 'the big merry Irish priests are a delight': he thought that they were like 'big children & all over six feet'. They 'were delighted to talk about Ireland' and happy to sit up late 'talking ghost stories' and 'drinking punch with me' ... 'I have been entirely delighted by the big merry priests of Notre Dame – all of them Irish & proud as Lucifer of their success in getting Jews and non-conformists to come to their college'.

Yeats was impressed by this tolerance as opposed to the rampant sectarianism which infected university life in Ireland;

> Certainly I have been astonished at one thing the general lack of religious prejudice I found on all sides here. At the Catholic university of Notre Dame, in Indiana, where all the professors are priests, I found about 100 non-conformists and I was told that a Jew had just carried off the prize in Christian Doctrine. This problem as others America has solved very efficiently.

Fr. Cavanaugh, about to assume the Presidency of Notre Dame, recalls the occasion slightly differently:

> Yeats was an inexhaustible source of delight. I've never known anyone so forgetful of little details. Whenever it came time for his lecture in Washington Hall on the campus, he seized his portfolio and marched over only to find after he arrived on the stage that he had brought the wrong lecture or no lecture at all in an empty portfolio. This was constantly happening. Similarly he would go out into the cold winter weather without a hat and after four or five minutes he would remember that he was hatless and hurry back to his room to get a covering for his head. The number of experiences of this kind was almost endless. At last it came time for him to go away and as I bade him good-bye and waved to him as the

Yeats and Fr. Charles O'Donnell, CSC, President of Notre Dame, 1933.

University of Notre Dame

SOUTH BEND, INDIANA

FRIDAY, JANUARY 10, 1913

Noon until 2:00 o'clock

A Special Performance in the Theatre of the University by

The Irish Players

from the Abbey Theatre, Dublin

The Liebler Company . . . . . American Manager
Mr. Frederick Donaghey . . . for the Liebler Company
(The Performance by Courtesy of The Chicago Theatre Society.)

Program of Three Plays

starting with

"KATHLEEN-NI-HOULIHAN"

A Play, in One Act, by William Butler Yeats. Cast Thus:

PETER GILLANE . . . . . Mr. J. A. O'ROURKE
PATRICK GILLANE . . . . . . Mr. U. WRIGHT
MICHAEL GILLANE . . . . . Mr. J. M. KERRIGAN
BRIDGET GILLANE . . . . Miss EILEEN O'DOHERTY
KATHLEEN-NI-HOULIHAN . . . . Miss SARA ALLGOOD
DELIA CAHEL . . . . Miss EITHNE MaGEE

The period is 1798. The setting is Peter Gillane's cottage near Killala.

"One night I had a dream, almost as distinct as a vision, of a cottage where there was well-being, and fire-light, and talk of marriage; and into the midst of that cottage there came an old woman, in a long cloak. She was Ireland, herself—that Kathleen-ni-Houlihan for whom so many songs have been sung, and for whose sake so many have gone to their death. I thought, if I could write this out as a little play, I could make others see my dream as I had seen it."—W. B. Yeats.

followed by

"THE RISING OF THE MOON"

A Play, in One Act, by Lady Gregory. Cast Thus:

A SERGEANT . . . . Mr. ARTHUR SINCLAIR
POLICEMAN X . . . . Mr. J. A. O'ROURKE
POLICEMAN B . . . . Mr. U. WRIGHT
A BALLAD-SINGER . . . . . Mr. J. M. KERRIGAN

The setting is a quay-side in a seaport.

ending with

"THE WORKHOUSE-WARD"

A Comedy, in One Act, by Lady Gregory. Cast Thus:

MIKE MACINERNEY } . paupers . { Mr. ARTHUR SINCLAIR
MICHAEL MISKELL } . paupers . { Mr. J. M. KERRIGAN
MRS. DONOGHUE . . . . Miss EILEEN O'DOHERTY

The setting is a ward in the Cloon Workhouse.

The poster advertising the Abbey Theatre's performance at Notre Dame, 1913.

> automobile trundled on out of sight, I said to someone near me: 'I wonder what he has forgotten now'. Three minutes after as I still stood watching the departing guest, I saw the machine turn round about the graveyard and scurry back to the entrance to the Administration Building where I was standing. I waited leisurely guessing what had happened. As he bounded out of the car and up the steps I said to him: 'Well, Mr. Yeats, what have you forgotten now?' 'Upon my soul, Father,' he said, 'I've forgot my teeth'. He dashed anxiously into his old bedroom and returned in a moment, triumphant and with his teeth.

However, Yeats's initial visit to Notre Dame had one unexpected and hugely positive result. He learned that the students had just staged Sophocles' great play *Oedipus Rex* and this inspired him to translate and stage Sophocles himself. The seed at Notre Dame finally blossomed in the 1920s, when Yeats staged *King Oedipus* in the Abbey in 1926 and *Oedipus at Colonus* in 1927. His contact with Notre Dame had produced brilliant fruit two decades later.

Yeats also encouraged the Abbey Theatre to visit Notre Dame in 1913 on their American Tour. On 10 January, they performed three one-act plays in 'the theatre of the university': Yeats's *Kathleen-Ni-Houlihan*, and Lady Gregory's *The Rising of the Moon* and *The Workhouse Ward*. Among the actors appearing in Washington Hall was Sara Allgood, beloved of the dramatist John Millington Synge and a mainstay of the early Abbey.

Yeats returned to campus for his second visit in 1933. The then President Father O'Donnell wrote:

> [Yeats] came in yesterday with a wild-eyed secretary, a Captain Duncan from Dublin, and they left at noon today ... The fellow, by the way, is positively 'hipped' on psychical research, but on the whole he was much more human and agreeable than the somewhat snobbish and esoteric freak that he appeared to me thirty years ago.

DE VALERA AT NOTRE DAME 1919

Once the Irish writers started coming to campus, the politicians soon followed. Éamon De Valera visited campus on his American whistle-stop tour of 1919. He was trying to sway American opinion back behind the Irish cause after the reputational damage inflicted when the USA entered the First World War. Irish-Americans had been supporting the Germans (on the grounds that England's enemy was Ireland's friend) and they found themselves badly wrong-footed when America joined the war on the British side. In 1916 President Woodrow Wilson had criticised 'the poison of disloyalty' within the immigrant community because of their continuing passion for the politics of their homelands, singling out the Irish as 'creatures of passion, loyalty and anarchy'. Wilson failed to do anything for Ireland in the Versailles Treaty after World War I, a war ostensibly fought to safeguard the rights of small nations.

De Valera, senior surviving leader of the 1916 Rising, and newly escaped from a British jail, embarked on a coast-to-coast tour of the USA in 1919–1920. Using the title 'President of Ireland', he criss-crossed America from New York to San Francisco by plane, boat and train, speaking to over one million people at iconic venues like Madison Square Garden and Fenway Park, and raising five million dollars for the cause of Irish independence.

De Valera's primary purpose was to restore the tarnished image of Ireland in American eyes. Counteracting the dangerous perception that Irish-Americans were disloyal, he stressed that Irish blood had flowed copiously in every battle that America had ever fought, reaching right back to the War of Independence, and commented acerbically that after the First World War, 'Ireland was a squeezed lemon and cast aside'. Playing the race card, he also noted that Ireland was 'the only white nation on the earth still in the bonds of political slavery'.

De Valera arrived at Notre Dame on 15 October 1919. A gigantic version of UND spelled out by 1,600 students in formation greeted him, as the students constantly chanted his name. De Valera ostentatiously laid a wreath before the statue of Father William Corby, with a card reading: 'From Éamon de Valera in loving tribute to Father Corby, who gave general absolution to the Irish Brigade at Gettysburg'. The canny Irish politician was deliberately invoking the memory of the 'Fighting Irish' and their great sacrifices on behalf of America during the Civil War. De Valera then inspected the 'Gaelic Collection' in the library, including the sword of 'Meagher of the Sword', Thomas Francis Meagher, General in the Irish Brigade.

De Valera planted a tree to mark his visit, before speaking at Washington Hall, where twelve hundred students were packed

Éamon de Valera on the Notre Dame campus, 1919.

in. De Valera launched a searing attack on malign British influence in Ireland: 'Seventy years ago, our population was five-eights that of England. She considered this a menace too grave to be allowed to continue and by persistent oppression she has succeeded in reducing our population by half'. He justified the 1916 Rising: 'Our rising was not really a rebellion but simply another battle in a long-continued fight which has never been given up. Secondly, the object of war is not always simply to beat the enemy in the field. The object in the main is the acquiring of a political result'.

The University gave him 'one of the greatest ovations that Notre Dame has ever accorded a visitor' and De Valera described it as his 'happiest day since coming to America'. But even within the welcoming campus of Notre Dame, acrimony lurked: the tree that De Valera had planted mysteriously disappeared.

Fifty years later, President De Valera repaid the hospitality when he invited the touring Notre Dame rugby team to visit him in 1968 in his official residence, Áras an Uachtaráin. The team played five games, losing to Navan, Delvin and University College Cork but beating Limerick Rovers and Thurles.

The links with Ireland remained strong until the Second World War. For example, Desmond Fitzgerald, poet, 1916 leader, Irish government minister, and father of Garret (a future Taoiseach), taught philosophy at Notre Dame from 1935 to 1941. He was described by Fr. Arthur Hope, CSC, as 'the best liked, both for his solid thought and dexterity of speech' among visiting lecturers. One of his hidden legacies is the fine collection of Irish books from this period to be found in the Hesburgh Library.

In more recent years, a constant stream of distinguished Irish people have visited the campus, ranging from writers

President De Valera greets the ND rugby team, 1968.

such as Seamus Heaney, Edna O'Brien, John MacGahern, Patrick McCabe, Paul Muldoon and Nuala Ní Dhomnaill, to musicians and dancers like U2, Altan, Jean Butler and the Chieftains, to presidents like Mary Robinson and Mary McAleese, Taoisigh such as Garret Fitzgerald and Enda Kenny, politicians like Gerry Adams, archbishops like Diarmuid Martin and sporting legends like Brian Mullins.

The continuing esteem in which Notre Dame is held in Ireland is attested by the granting of honorary Irish citizenship to two leading figures in the modern history of the university: Don Keough in 2007 and Fr. Ted Hesburgh in 2012. Hesburgh's Irish roots emanate from his mother Anne Marie Murphy. Her father, Martin Murphy, left Wexford in Ireland as an eighteen-month old infant in 1857. Hesburgh, born in 1917, grew up in an Irish neighbourhood in Syracuse, N.Y. and always credited his mother with imparting a strong sense of Irishness to him: 'My mother was a very Irish woman. I always thought I am more like my mother than my father, who was of Luxembourgish decent'.

Hesburgh, who served as president of ND from 1952 to 1987, is widely credited with elevating ND into a great American university with an international reputation for excellence. Speaking at the ceremony on St. Patrick's Day 2012 where Hesburgh received Irish citizenship, Don Keough (whose ancestors also came from County Wexford) described him as 'the soul of this place'. Though among the most garlanded of Americans (he had sixteen appointments from American presidents and retains the Guinness Book of Records title for 'most honorary degrees', with 150), the 95 year-old Hesburgh considered his Irish citizenship and passport to be among the highest honours that he had ever received.

Fr. Ted Hesburgh, CSC, links arms with Martin Luther King in a Civil Rights rally at Soldiers' Field Chicago in 1964 (*South Bend Tribune*, 21 June 1964).

Everybody who's anybody has been to Notre Dame...': U2 pray at the Grotto with Fr. Tim Scully, CSC. They played at ND's Joyce Centre on 10 October 2001.

Taoiseach Enda Kenny with Vice Admiral Michael Miller, Superintendent of the U.S. Naval Academy, and ND Dublin representative Joseph Stranix in Washington, March 2012 promoting the ND/Navy game to be held on 1 September 2012.

From the Heart: Kevin Whelan, Smurfit Director of the Keough Naughton Notre Dame Centre, Dublin

Many Americans come back to Ireland to seek the graves of their ancestors. Every time that I visit Notre Dame, I make a reverse trip, as my grand-uncle Brother Aidan O'Reilly, CSC (1877–1948) is buried in the peaceful Holy Cross cemetery on campus. I am always aware of Brother Aidan's presence there and I never leave the campus without visiting his grave. I am proud that our family connection to ND has been re-established since I started working for the University in 1998.

Patrick and Margaret O'Reilly of Bunclody, County Wexford, were the parents of Brother Aidan, whose Christian name was Thomas. Patrick was a highly skilled wet cooper – capable of making leak-proof barrels, used for packing salmon and butter. Their parish priest described the O'Reillys as 'respectable and excellent parents and devout Catholics'.

Thomas was born in 1877 and had two brothers, Myles, and my grandfather Patrick ('Park'). Brother Aidan's father died in 1882 when he was only five years old. His uncle Myles took over the cooperage and responsibility for the family. The boys attended the infant school at the Faithful Companions of Jesus Convent in Bunclody. The two younger boys, Myles and Patrick, were apprenticed to their uncle as coopers but Thomas continued his education. A further tragedy was that his mother Margaret died in 1894, following the bite of a dog. She was only forty-two years old, and her death orphaned the three teenagers.

In 1899, Thomas met a distant relative Rev. Andrew Morrissey, CSC (1860–1921), the seventh President of Notre Dame (1893–1905). He was born in Thomastown, County Kilkenny, although he presumably had some connection to the well-known Morrissey family of Bunclody. Fr. Morrissey was a potent figure in Irish-America; he was involved with the influential Friends of Irish Freedom, and he championed Irish matters at Notre Dame. Fr. Morrissey recruited Thomas O'Reilly to the CSC congregation.

Thomas left Ireland in Summer 1899 to seek a new world in a new setting in a new century. What courage that required. His file at the Notre Dame Archives lists his next of kin as Patrick O'Reilly of 'Johnstown Cottage' – the townland where I was born. Brother Aidan travelled by ship to New York and then by train to the American mid-west. He always stated that he fell in love with Notre Dame at his first sight of the Golden Dome. There was at least one thing on campus that reminded him of home: in 1902, a thirty acre field of reassuringly familiar potatoes occupied the space where the old Post Office and University Club used to stand.

He was inducted into the Congregation of the Holy Cross on 15 August 1899, an appropriate date for an institution devoted to Our Lady. He chose the highly appropriate name of Aidan, Bishop of Ferns, his natal diocese. He took his final religious vows in 1902. In 1906 he was named first director of ND's new hall of studies for the Christian

Brothers – now known as the First College Building. He also wrote two of the first vocation manuals for the CSC: *The Gateway to the Religious Life* and *Out of Many Hearts*. The Irish writer Seamus MacManus described him in 1917 as 'Brother Aidan of the beautiful character, noble representative of the noble land to which his warm heart, ever turning, is needle-true'.

His notebooks from his novitiate years survive and reveal wide reading in both spiritual and literary works. One of the people whose lectures he attended was W. B. Yeats in Washington Hall in January 1904. 'I followed the lecture from start to finish with keen interest'. He noted that Yeats's 'gestures are often stiff and ill-timed. On the stage he strikes you as very unassuming and not a bit self-centered' but he concluded that 'Yeats had one of the requisites of a true orator – sincerity – but he hasn't the gift of the gab'.

Brother Aidan developed a lifelong habit of taking notes. Years later in the National Library of Ireland, I found the following quotation that I have never forgotten in one of the books on Wexford history that he later donated to the Library: 'The faintest of inks is more retentive than the strongest of memories'. He had taken a vow of poverty and he never sought funds to go back to visit Ireland: he only did so once when he stayed at the Faithful Companions of Jesus Convent where he had been a pupil so many years before, and which I myself was later to attend in the 1970s.

Brother Aidan was keen to expand Holy Cross education into the American high school system and he undertook further studies to earn the appropriate qualifications. In 1909, the CSC opened their first high school. In 1919, he was appointed President of Holy Cross College in New Orleans, a high school that combined a boarding and day element. He taught English and Math. Later he was transferred to teach in high schools in Evansville, Fort Wayne, South Bend and Indianapolis. Then he moved back to campus to teach English at ND and to become the archivist.

He died there on 19 February 1948, and is buried in the serried ranks of his beloved CSC community, close to the grotto. A Wexfordman had come to rest in northern Indiana. A memorial pamphlet was written on his life entitled *As a Star for All Eternity*. The title pays tribute to those who choose the vocation of teaching: 'Those that instruct many to justice shall shine as stars for all eternity' [Daniel 12:3].

A giant banner drapes Carroll Hall on the ND campus.

ND Spring 2011 in Connemara.

4
CHAPTER

IRISH STUDIES AT NOTRE DAME

IRISH STUDIES AT NOTRE DAME

Ireland is so small that if you picked it up and dropped it in the Atlantic Ocean, you might have to spend a long time looking for it. Yet the island has an extraordinary tradition in literature in at least two languages, a unique role in relation to British and European historical development, and a disproportionate influence on the history of the United States. Britain's oldest colony, it became one of the world's newest post-colonial states when it achieved independence from the British Empire. In recent years, it has seen the evolution of a Peace Process which has slowly but surely transformed Northern Ireland. The Republic has witnessed the spectacular rise and fall of the Celtic Tiger, and turbulent relationships with the EU and the euro project. Simultaneously, the country experienced substantial immigration, transforming a monolithic culture through the introduction of the 'New Irish' with their varied languages and cultures.

One of the most rapid economic and social transformations experienced anywhere in the world has also occurred in this generation, marked most obviously by the dramatic weakening of the public role of Catholicism, the rise of Dublin as a global city, and the emergence of the Irish economy as among the most open in the world. Ireland and America have also re-engaged in multiple ways, signalled by the presence of one thousand US firms in Ireland. The Irish economy, despite the stunning banking and property crash, remains among the most globalised in the world, the European headquarters of hundreds of the world's leading companies. Contemporary Ireland is a laboratory for the study of the impact of globalisation on a vernacular culture, a hybridised world where tradition and modernity are not opposites but co-partners, and home to an always challenging but never boring society.

Notre Dame is an appropriate home for one of the world's leading Irish Studies programmes, given its intense historical connection with Irish-America and Ireland. The Keough-Naughton Institute of Irish Studies, through its wide array of committed teachers and researchers, offers Notre Dame students a unique opportunity to explore Ireland's extraordinary tradition in literature (in both the English and Irish languages), its distinctive historical trajectory, and its abiding influence on the United States.

The core programme is a Minor in Irish Studies, which allows students to deepen their understanding of Ireland across a variety of disciplines, including English, Irish Language and Literature, History, Anthropology, Film, Theatre and Television. In this way, mentored by gifted professors, they study Irish literature, society, culture and politics through both course work and increasingly through first-hand experience of Ireland. A growing suite of internship opportunities, field-courses on the Irish West coast, language immersion in Connemara, and access to the Dublin programme all provide direct contact with the culture outside the confines of the classroom. Thanks to generous support from benefactors, the ND campus is also able to attract a steady stream of high-calibre Irish speakers, who ensure that the intellectual bloodstream of Ireland flows though the veins of Notre Dame.

The most gratifying aspect of Irish Studies at Notre Dame is that our students have shown an enormous appetite for the multiple and diverse courses on offer. 'Build it and they will come' was what Don Keough presciently suggested back in 1993; the current vigorous health of Irish Studies on the campus is proof of how right he was. The Keough-Naughton Institute has also enjoyed sustained support from the university leadership, who see it is an important component of Notre Dame's impressive drive towards sustained academic achievement, and its ambition to be world-class. Since the Institute was established, it is increasingly acknowledged across the board that Notre Dame has ascended to a position of global leadership in the field of Irish Studies. The Keough-Naughton Institute has garnered considerable attention in the scholarly world, as well as recognition from the National Endowment for the Humanities, the Fulbright Commission, the *New York Times*, the *Chronicle of Higher Education*, and more than one hundred media outlets worldwide.

The History department at Notre Dame hosts three Irish Studies scholars. Jim Smyth joined in 1995, and he was followed in 2009 by Rory Rapple. A dedicated Madden Hennebry chair was established in 2008 to promote the study of Irish-American history. Patrick Griffin was named the Madden-Hennebry Professor in 2008 and Chair of the History Department in 2011. His work explores the intersection of colonial American and early modern Irish and British history. It focuses on

Atlantic-wide themes and dynamics. He has published work on the movement of peoples and cultures across the Atlantic Ocean, as well as the process of adaptation. Griffin examines the ways in which Ireland, Britain, and America were linked – and differed – during the seventeenth and eighteenth centuries. He has looked at revolution and rebellion, movement and migration, and colonisation and violence in each society in comparative perspective. Among his publications are *The People with No Name: Ireland's Ulster Scots, America's Scots Irish, and the Creation of a British Atlantic World* (2001), *American Leviathan: Empire, Nation, and Revolutionary Frontier* (2007) and *America's Revolution* (2012).

Notre Dame's English Department hosts Irish Studies scholars Christopher Fox (1986), Susan Cannon Harris (1998), Mary Burgess (1999), Declan Kiberd (2011) and Barry McCrea (2012). Declan Kiberd, described by the *Chronicle of Higher Education* as 'one of Ireland's most prominent intellectuals' and 'a leading literary scholar', was appointed Donald and Marilyn Keough Professor of Irish Studies in 2011. He teaches Irish literature and culture to students at the Notre Dame campus each fall and in the Keough Naughton Dublin Centre each spring and summer. Kiberd, a Dubliner, previously taught at University College Dublin from 1979 to 2010. Edward Said praised his *Inventing Ireland: Literature of the Modern Nation* (1996) as 'a highly readable, joyfully contentious book' of 'enormous learning and superb understanding'. Professor Kiberd has lectured on Irish literature in more than thirty countries, and he has been a Visiting Professor of Irish literature at several universities, including Columbia, Cambridge, Duke, and the Sorbonne. He is author of eight books and over one hundred articles and essays on Irish writers in the English and Irish languages. His book *Irish Classics* (2000) won the Truman Capote Prize for the best work of literary criticism in the English-speaking world.

Announcing Kiberd's appointment, Christopher Fox, Director of the Keough-Naughton Institute, said: 'his presence on the Notre Dame faculty reinforces our position as the world leader in Irish Studies for years to come'. Kiberd welcomed the interdisciplinary focus and English-Irish language emphasis in Irish Studies at Notre Dame: 'I have always been amphibious. I work both in Irish and in English, so this is a great attraction for me, to have students working on the cusp between both languages, and also to be working on the cusp with such disciplines as history, sociology, and political science'.

The swelling cohort of graduate students attracted to the Keough-Naughton Institute by its stellar faculty generally complete doctorates in History, English and Literature. The Irish holdings in the Hesburgh Library can sustain advanced research in all areas of Irish society and culture. Each graduate student is encouraged to learn the Irish language, and there are funded opportunities to study the language in Ireland through a joint programme with NUI Galway. Students who wish to pursue a graduate degree with an Irish language and literature focus can do so through the Ph.D. in Literature Program.

A Department of Irish Language and Literature within the Keough-Naughton Institute was officially launched on 1 October 2004 – the first dedicated Department of Irish Language and Literature in the United States. The department copper-fastens the Institute's commitment to the

Declan Kiberd speaking at O'Connell House.

Irish novelist Patrick McCabe performs at Notre Dame.

Irish language and recognises Irish as a core component of the discipline of Irish Studies. Since his arrival on campus in 1994, Peter McQuillan has presided over the phenomenal growth of students taking Irish classes at Notre Dame and assisted in building up the unrivalled Irish-language collection in the Hesburgh Library.

In 2003, Breandán Ó Buachalla, widely regarded as the leading Irish-language scholar in the world, became the first Thomas & Kathleen O'Donnell Chair of Irish in the Keough-Naughton Institute. Under his stewardship, the Department of Irish Language and Literature was founded. In 2003, 120 undergraduate and graduate students were taking Irish language classes (by comparison, 95 took Russian and 135 took Japanese during the same period). With new recruits Sarah McKibben (2002) and Brian Ó Conchubhair (2004), the Institute was able to launch the first minor in Irish Language & Literature in North America through the new department.

The fledgling Department has been subsequently augmented by the addition of distinguished faculty Tara Áine MacLeod (2005) and Diarmuid Ó Giolláin (2010). In 2008, Bríona Nic Dhiarmada was appointed the Thomas J. & Kathleen O'Donnell Chair of Irish Language & Literature and Concurrent Professor of Film, Television, and Theatre. She first came to campus as the Naughton Distinguished Visiting Professor in Spring 2006. During the same semester, in 2006, her critical book on the poet Nuala Ní Dhomhnaill, *Teacs Baineann, Teacs Mná,* won the prestigious Merriman Prize for Irish Language Academic Book of the Year. She is an editor of *The Field Day Anthology,* co-editor of *Téacs agus comhthéacs: Gnéithe de chritic na Gaeilge,* and general editor of the forthcoming *Cambridge History of Irish Women Writers.* A distinguished documentary filmmaker and screenwriter, Bríona is the author of over thirty-five screenplays and ten documentaries. She won the 2007 Television Programme of the Year at Oireachtas na Gaeilge. She is currently working on a major multi-part documentary series on the Easter Rising of 1916, which will be broadcast on public television internationally.

The numbers of students in Irish classes continued to grow. The Department has attracted the support of the Fulbright Commission, who facilitate the presence on the ND campus of young Irish scholars who help teach the language. By 2012, Notre Dame had over four hundred students enrolled in Irish-language courses.

In 2012, Irish Studies at Notre Dame exceeded one thousand undergraduates and twenty-five graduate students were taking institute-cross-listed courses each semester in the Departments of Anthropology, English, Film, Television and Theater, Irish Language and Literature, and Political Science. Other distinguished faculty in Irish Studies includes Fr. Sean McGraw, CSC, who joined the Political Science department in 2009, and Ian Kujit, who joined the Anthropology department in 2001. Deceased faculty include John Darby, Professor of Peace Studies, who was a joint Fellow of the Keough-Naughton and Kroc Institutes from 2000 to 2012. Irish Studies on campus has also been enriched by a stream of visiting Professors, including John Kelly, Tom Bartlett, Ciarán Brady, Angela Bourke, Nuala Ní Dhomhnaill, Patrick McCabe, P. J. Mathews, Diarmuid Ó Doibhlin, Gearóid Ó Crualaíoch and Nicholas Canny.

THE FOUNDERS OF IRISH STUDIES AT ND: SEAMUS DEANE AND CHRISTOPHER FOX

Don Keough made a $2.5-million gift to the University to get the programme started in 1993. At that time, Seamus Deane became the first head of Irish Studies at Notre Dame. Identified by Christopher Fox, then chair of ND's English Department, as the best person to lead the proposed Irish Studies initiative on campus, Deane was persuaded by Fox and Provost Nathan Hatch to accept the challenge. Deane set out to ensure that the Irish Studies programme at Notre Dame would deal with writing from the 1,500-year span of Irish literary history, in Irish as well as English – not just 'the Golden Oldies'. This ambition to be comprehensive and to address both Irish and English language literature set Deane's project apart. So did his determination to build in-depth library holdings at a level sufficient to nurture a wide range of exemplary scholarship.

Speaking to the *Chronicle of Higher Education* on 15 December 1993, the then Berkeley-based scholar David Lloyd identified Deane as 'clearly the principal Irish intellectual at the moment' while Christopher Fox called Deane 'the top Joyce scholar in the world'. Deane sought to give the ND programme 'some particular distinction' because of his belief that 'Irish Studies leads a very exiguous life, as an appendix, sometimes a diseased appendix, to British or English literature'. Deane also wanted to challenge the prevalent American view of Ireland that 'is so confined, and in many ways so anorexic'.

Seamus Deane c. 1980

Seamus Deane's work had consistently interrogated 'Irishness', in a stream of elegantly written essays – almost one hundred – and books that disrupted lazy notions about the country. Deane's scholarship ranged from Jonathan Swift and Edmund Burke, to W. B. Yeats, and James Joyce, from Samuel Beckett and Flann O'Brien to his friends Brian Friel and Seamus Heaney.

Deane is often described as the most intelligent person in Ireland and – to his amusement – his American visa recognises him as 'an alien of extraordinary ability'. As well as an unrivalled fluency in thought and speech, Deane possesses that rarest of gifts – a genuinely photographic memory. His lectures are delivered extempore – aided at most by three or four words written on a tiny page. Yet they will soar, range widely, be coherent and make anyone listening feel they are seriously deficient in wider cultural knowledge. Deane's range of reference is astonishing: from opera and classical music to American literature, from obscure seventeenth-century philosophers to contemporary detective fiction, from the most arcane 'Theory' to the fortunes of Glasgow Celtic, from French *auteur* films to Moore's melodies, or, as he might himself say, from the banausic to the sublime.

Seamus Deane was born in 1940 in the Bogside in Derry, on the border between north and south. A promising career as a stylish soccer player was terminated by a bad knee injury. For centuries, the Bogside had been a festering Catholic slum, as described by Deane:

> The Bogside and its neighbouring streets lay flat on the floor of a narrowed valley. Above it towards Belfast rose the walls, the Protestant cathedral, the pillared statue of Governor Walker [Protestant hero of the siege of Derry in 1690], the whole apparatus of Protestant domination. History shadowed our faces. Behind us rose the middle-class Catholic quarters, no Bogsiders in those days. The drifting aromas of poverty were pungent and constant reminders to the inhabitants of those upper heights that if the Protestant Ascendancy was justified by the freaks of history, class distinction had the merciful support of geography. We lived below and between.

Deane attended St. Columb's College in Derry. He was among the first cohort of Catholics in Northern Ireland to be able to proceed to university, earning a BA in 1961 and MA in 1963 from Queen's University Belfast. Deane himself has commented:

> We were the first generation to benefit from the post war educational reforms of the Labour government. My father said, 'Educate yourself, I wish I had the chance. That's the way to resist'. There was poverty, gerrymandering, discrimination, a failed political system ... a great sense of isolation ... but no way to mobilise the anger; I felt as though I was living in a frozen sea.

Deane completed his doctorate at Cambridge in 1966, and he then taught English literature for two years at Reed College and Berkeley in the United States. He returned to Ireland to lecture at University College Dublin from 1968 to 1980 where he was then appointed professor of Modern English and American literature. Deane also spent a semester teaching at Notre Dame in 1973, where among his best students was Joe Montana. Deane is a poet of distinction, with three published collections. He attended school with Seamus Heaney, shared an apartment with him when they went to Queens together, and remained an influential mentor over the years as his friend's career soared. In 1980, Deane joined Field Day, founded by the dramatist Brian Friel and the actor Stephen Rea. The group staged a series of

Seamus Heaney with Iseult and Seamus Deane, 2011.

impressive plays across the island and Deane added an acerbic and incisive intellectual edge to its activities.

Deane, already highly regarded as a poet, now concentrated his energies on scholarly interests, marked by the rapid publication of *Celtic Revivals* (1985), *A Short History of Irish Literature* (1986) and *The French Revolution and Enlightenment in England* (1988) – his doctoral thesis in book form. During the early 1990s, he edited the transformative *Field Day Anthology of Irish Writing* (1991), as well as a six-volume edition of Joyce's works for the Penguin Twentieth-Century Classics series, a deliberate project to reclaim Joyce as an Irish writer. Deane enjoyed an international reputation: Edward Said, for example, widely regarded as the founder of post-colonialism, invited him to give the key-note lecture at a conference celebrating Said's career at his own Columbia University.

Deane's novel, *Reading in the Dark*, largely written at Notre Dame, appeared in 1996. It is recognised as a modern classic, the most insightful novel written about the Troubles, and marked by all of Deane's intelligence, wit and sly quotation from, and allusion to, a vast range of Irish literature. Because it is written in the deceptively accessible *bildungsroman* style, the Gothic, post-modern and post-colonial thrust of this powerful novel has been insufficiently understood.

Seamus Deane led Irish Studies at Notre Dame from 1993 to 2004. He continued to teach in the Keough Naughton Centre in Dublin from 2004, in both the undergraduate programme and the graduate Irish Seminar. In a collaborative Field Day/Keough-Naughton Institute venture, he has also run a highly regarded publishing operation in Dublin, whose flagship publication since 2005 has been the annual *Field Day Review*.

CHRISTOPHER FOX

Deane's co-founder of the Irish Studies project at Notre Dame was Christopher Fox, then chair of the Department of English. It was Fox who identified Deane as the right person to take up the reins of Irish Studies at Notre Dame and to drive it forward. He also enthused Provost Nathan Hatch and Don Keough about the concept, and together the Keough/Fox/Hatch axis was able to persuade Deane to head up Notre

Reading in the Dark editions.

Dame's proposed operation. From the beginning, no-one had higher intellectual ambitions for the project than Christopher Fox, and it was really his desire for excellence that made everything possible. Together Deane and Fox made a highly effective partnership, with Fox's drive, energy and capacity to get things done gelling perfectly with Deane's strategic vision and formidable intellectual prowess. The duo at the head of Irish Studies elicited strong support from the university leadership in advancing the project, and Irish Studies at Notre Dame very quickly entered a remarkable growth trajectory. There can be no doubt that this trajectory was fuelled by Fox's ferocious energy, enthusiasm and demand for high quality. He made all the hard yards.

Christopher Fox received his doctorate from SUNY-Binghamton where he won the Distinguished Dissertation in the Humanities and Fine Arts Prize. His interests in Irish Studies grew out of his work on eighteenth-century literature, especially his growing interest in Jonathan Swift. A tribute to his wider scholarly standing, Fox has held fellowships from the National Endowment for the Humanities, the American Council of Learned Societies, the Newberry Library, and the Folger Institute. Fox has served on the national board of the American Society for Eighteenth-Century Studies and the editorial boards of various journals, including *Eighteenth-Century Studies* and *Bullan: A Journal of Irish Studies.*

At Notre Dame, Fox has served in various leadership positions, including acting Dean of Arts and Letters. When he was appointed inaugural Director of the Keough Institute for Irish Studies in 2001, it merely gave formal recognition to a role he had played from the beginning. Fox is the author of *Locke and the Scriblerians: Identity and Consciousness in Eighteenth-Century Britain* (1988). He has edited *Psychology and Literature in the Eighteenth Century* (1987), *Teaching Eighteenth-Century Poetry* (1990), *Gulliver's Travels: Text and Case Studies in Contemporary Criticism* (1995), *Inventing Human Science: Eighteenth-Century Domains* (1995), and *The Cambridge Companion to Jonathan Swift* (2003).

BREANDÁN Ó BUACHALLA (1936–2010)

If Seamus Deane and Christopher Fox were the founders of the Irish Studies programme at Notre Dame, Breandán Ó Buachalla was the principal founder of the Department of Irish Language and Literature. Ó Buachalla became the inaugural Thomas J. and Kathleen O'Donnell Chair of Irish

Breandán Ó Buachalla.

Language and Literature at Notre Dame in 2003, an endowed chair especially established for him. He was immensely proud of the fact that during his period at the helm in Notre Dame, he founded the first modern Irish language department to be established outside Ireland. Breandán was especially pleased to be able to teach doctoral seminars in Irish.

His time at Queens University Belfast was the basis of his first – and still authoritative – book, *I mBéal Feirste Cois Cuain* (1968, 1978), a study of scribal and antiquarian circles in Belfast. He became an authority on the Ulster poets, notably Peadar Ó Doirnín and Cathal Buí Mac Giolla Ghunna. In Belfast, he deepened his life-long interest in Scottish culture, and he always stressed the natural affinity between Irish and Scots Gaelic, working actively to promote scholarly and cultural links. He maintained that Gaelic Ulster naturally accepted Scotland as an extension of itself.

He published on an impressively broad spectrum of topics: the literature and ideology of early modern Ireland, the impact of the Counter-Reformation on Irish political thought, early modern Irish historiography, linguistics,

Gaelic poetry, and the cult of the Stuarts in Irish literature. Above all, he was an expert on Jacobitism and for decades tracked this ideology systematically through an impressively broad range of manuscripts. His magisterial statement *Aisling Ghéar: na Stíobhartaigh agus an tAos Léinn 1603-1788* (1996) placed Ó Buachalla in the pantheon of great Irish scholars – the company of O'Donovan and O'Curry, Zeuss and Marstrander. He would have been happy to be considered among 'the manuscript men', that venerable tradition of Irish language scholarship rooted in the manuscripts themselves.

Breandán Ó Buachalla was a champion of the language not just in scholarship but in advocacy. He spoke Munster Irish in an expressive, idiomatic and always elegant way. He conducted extensive linguistic fieldwork on Cape Clear Island off the Cork coast and he adored Corca Dhuibhne, spending many summers there in the heart of the living language. He campaigned arduously to keep Dún Chaoin national school open after its scandalous closure in 1970. In 1973, it was formally reopened and still functions successfully today. Through his broadcasting, journalism and public lecturing, he contributed generously to the creation of a public sphere in Ireland that would be enriched by the heritage and values of the Irish-speaking community.

Breandán never ceased to be engaged in new scholarly projects. He edited two beautifully produced and meticulously edited volumes in the Field Day series on the works of the eighteenth-century poets, Aogán Ó Rathaille and Eoghan Rua Ó Súilleabháin. He admired the sophisticated metrics and technical prowess of the Munster poets, and delighted in reading or reciting their poems from memory. He knew all of 'Caoineadh Airt Uí Laoghaire' by heart. He had the natural generosity of all true scholars, and he was held in vast affection by his many graduate students, who got to know the warm private man behind the erudite public face. Brendán Ó Buachalla died in 2010 in a medical misadventure, to the enduring sorrow of his family, friends and colleagues.

IRELAND COUNCIL MEMBERS 2012

The Ireland Council and Irish Studies faculty, Merrion Hotel, Dublin 2004.

Fergal and Rachael Naughton.

NOTRE DAME'S IRELAND COUNCIL

Notre Dame maintains advisory councils for its principal academic components to advance their development in the broadest context. Council members participate in that development in several ways. Through attendance at meetings, they acquire an understanding of the philosophy, plans, and priorities of the University. In turn, as members of Notre Dame's official family, they serve as representatives of the University in the cities where they reside and in their respective business and professional communities.

The Ireland Council draws together distinguished Irish and American leaders to support the university in its Irish Studies operation. Co-chaired by Donald Keough and Martin Naughton, the Council includes Irish-American corporate chieftains such as Andrew McKenna, John Madden, Philip Rooney, Kathleen Andrews, Tom O'Donnell and Richard Sweetman. The Council also has a young alum as a member. The Ireland Council normally meets at ND each October but it has also met in Dublin in 2002, 2004, 2008 and 2012.

Dick Sweetman, Christopher Fox, Kathy Sweetman and Niall O'Dowd, Stackallan, 2008.

IRISH COLLECTIONS AT THE HESBURGH LIBRARY

The Hesburgh Libraries sustain advanced research on all areas of Irish society and culture. They contain 3.3 million volumes, and enjoy an annual budget close to twenty million dollars. The Irish Studies material comprises impressive core collections, supplemented by purposeful purchasing. The Irish language has been the focus of serious recent attention. The Hesburgh's holdings include outstanding materials on the philosopher George Berkeley, the writers Jonathan Swift and Oliver Goldsmith, the politician Edmund Burke, and the poet James Clarence Mangan, as well as collections assembled by Captain Francis O'Neill on Irish music, Rolf and Magda Loeber on Irish fiction, and Risteárd Ó Glaisne on the Irish language. The early Irish print collection is strong on seventeenth and eighteenth-century Ireland, and there are extensive holdings relating to the 1798 Rising, the Great Famine and Irish-America, as well as on literature in Irish and English. Historically, the library is particularly rich in eighteenth-century Irish materials, with emerging concentrations in nineteenth and twentieth-century Irish literature.

Although considerably augmented in recent years, the collections' formation dates back to the mid-nineteenth century. The personal library of Captain Francis O'Neill, the Irish chief of police in Chicago, was among the early donations. O'Neill's library contains predictable riches on Irish music, in addition to leading scholarly and antiquarian books. Another impressive gift was the library of the Sweetmans of Clohamon House, County Wexford, a landowning Catholic family in nineteenth-century Ireland. This collection was donated generously by ND alumnus Richard Sweetman, a current member of the Ireland Council.

The Hesburgh Libraries swooped in 2003 to make a signature Irish Studies acquisition of the superb Loeber Collection of Irish Fiction. This unsurpassed set of Irish fiction published from 1650 to 1900 contains works by famous but more importantly obscure authors, embracing Irish-related fiction published in Britain, America and across the globe. The Loeber material gained even more attention with the 2006 publication of their *A Guide to Irish Fiction 1650-1900*. This restored to the horizon of scholarly visibility early Irish fiction that had fallen into virtual oblivion. The Loebers identified 1,455 Irish authors and provided thousands of encapsulated summaries of their works. The *Guide to Irish Fiction* details 5,889 pieces of Irish fiction published in Ireland, England, France, and North America, Australia and several other countries. No less than 2,444 of these titles were in the Loeber acquisition made by Notre Dame, instantly catapulting the university into pre-eminence as a global research centre on Irish fiction. The Library has continued to expand this core acquisition with the ambition of eventually housing the most comprehensive collection of Irish fiction in the world: the collection now numbers 4,000 volumes. This material is complemented by the Hesburgh holdings of rare broadside ballads: over five hundred Dublin-printed songs offer a unique insight into vernacular culture.

The Irish language material is impressive, particularly in twentieth-century literature and scholarship, with added depth through the purchase of the library of scholar Risteárd Ó Glaisne. The Hesburgh also holds the landmark early works of Irish language printing, much of it emanating from the Irish Catholic Colleges at Louvain and Paris in the seventeenth century. This collection offers impressive testimony to the intellectual virtuosity of the Irish Catholic diaspora. The more recent acquisition of the collection of the Celtic Studies scholar Charles Dunn further strengthens the Irish language materials. Twentieth-century Irish writing is another strength, offering one of the fullest collections of Irish fiction and drama in America.

Theatre history can be explored through a rare set of early Abbey Theatre programmes, the archive of the modern Belfast-based Charabanc Theatre, a unique set of Irish language plays in print, and volumes of plays produced in Dublin in the eighteenth and nineteenth centuries. This theatre material is enhanced by continual additions of contemporary scripts and screenplays by Irish writers, as well as of Irish films, and the Library offers guides to Irish films on its website.

Among the most visually attractive materials are those from the Cuala Press, including books, pamphlets, broadsides and greeting cards. Cuala, managed by the sisters of William Butler Yeats, enjoys a stellar reputation among the illustrious fine art presses of the world. Masterfully designed and beautifully printed, with many illustrations by Jack B. Yeats – yet another member of that talented family and widely regarded as the greatest Irish painter – the Cuala printings offer an

Rolf Loeber and Kevin Whelan examining Irish manuscripts.

indispensable insight into the extraordinary efflorescence of Irish culture known as the Irish Revival. This rich feast of visual material is supplemented by an outstanding set of Irish cartography donated by Thomas McGrath. Maps and charts, including valuable specimens by Speed and Mercator, were collected painstakingly over a fifty-year period.

St. Patrick at the Hill of Slane, Cuala Press.

While remaining committed to building superb print collections, the Hesburgh is also vigorously acquiring digital resources. Subscriptions to online archives and journals expand the holdings, while the ability to search multiple editions simultaneously has been enhanced through access to *Eighteenth Century Books Online, Early English Books Online* and other digital resources. The Hesburgh Libraries have focused on rare books and pamphlets, with concentrations in eighteenth-century history, augmented by digital and microfilm material. In this online age, improved access has also been prioritised, deploying innovative technology that allows microforms to be scanned directly onto computer files. The Irish Studies material now includes two thousand microfilm reels of Irish newspapers (often described as 'the first draft of history'), the Irish Catholic pamphlets from the Catholic University of America, and the magnificent Goldsmiths'-Kress Library of Economic Literature. The recent Troubles are covered in minute detail in *Northern Ireland Political Literature*, a microfilm set from Belfast's Linen Hall Library.

The Hesburgh Libraries pursue an aggressive acquisitions policy in Irish materials, one of the areas on which the university has staked its academic reputation. Under the impressive leadership of dedicated Irish Studies librarian Aedín Clements, these collections continue to grow from strength to strength.

CAPTAIN FRANCIS O'NEILL

Francis O'Neill (1848–1936) published the first major collections of Irish dance music. O'Neill was born at the height of the Famine in Tralibane, near Bantry in County Cork, the youngest of seven children. From an early age, O'Neill was a talented traditional flute player, with an impeccable memory and an expert musical ear. The teenager ran away to sea in 1865 and spent years as a sailor before he eventually settled down, In 1870, he married in Edina, Missouri. The great Chicago fire of 1871 stimulated a demand for construction workers and prompted a vast influx of Irish-Americans. O'Neill joined the Chicago police force in 1873, a favoured Irish-American occupation. He rose rapidly through the ranks to become superintendent of the Chicago Police Department from 1901 until his retirement as it's Chief in 1905.

O'Neill allegedly hired the Irish in his police force on the basis of whether they had musical talents or experience. In 1901, he was elected president of the Chicago Irish Music

Captain Francis O'Neill.

Club and he conceived of a ground-breaking project: transcribing traditional Irish music into sheet music form. As he himself could not read or write music, he recruited a musically literate collaborator, James O'Neill, to transcribe the pieces. O'Neill collected both the Irish music that he had heard growing up, as well as music from the Chicago Irish, especially in the Deering Street area. By 1900, there were over quarter of million Irish people in Chicago. On 2 March 1902, the *Chicago Sunday Tribune* reported that 'Chicago leads Ireland as a storehouse of Irish music'.

His first effort, *The Music of Ireland* (1903), contained 1,850 pieces: it attracted criticism that it contained too many tunes derived from non-traditional collections. The stung O'Neill culled these in his improved version in 1907 – *The Dance Music of Ireland*. This contained exclusively traditional Irish dance tunes, amounting to 1001 dance pieces. It was the most comprehensive collection of its kind, which quickly established itself as definitive for practicioners. 'O'Neills' is still the 'Bible of Irish Traditional Music' a century later. Its publication ensured the survival of the centuries-old traditional Irish airs.

O'Neill published five collections, as well as two books about his own life as a collector. He commissioned the first Irish language set of printer's type in America: 'Tools for engraving the modern Irish alphabet were manufactured in Chicago specially for this purpose'. He donated his manuscripts, recordings and correspondence to Notre Dame in 1931 and this archive is the largest collection of O'Neill's documents in the world. This included his personal library of 1,500 volumes on Ireland, which now forms 'The Captain Francis O'Neill Collection of Irish Music' in the Hesburgh Libraries. The collection also includes two manuscripts of tunes collected in Ireland by Henry Hudson in the 1830s and 1840s.

O'Neill chose Notre Dame because he believed that it offered a suitable home for Irish materials. He explained to President Charles O'Donnell, CSC in 1931: 'The spiritual atmosphere of Notre Dame is most favourable to the promotion of the donor's purpose ('to render this cherished collection of tomes available to scholars interested in the historic past of the homeland of the Gael'), so the renowned university has been selected as the repository of my literary treasure'.

From the Heart: Declan Kiberd, Donald and Marilyn Keough Professor of Irish Studies

The signs said 'Irish Way' or 'Waterford Drive' but when I arrived in mid-August the place didn't feel familiar at all. A hot Indiana light burned incessantly on fair skin, making me consider for the first time in my life the use of an umbrella for protection from the sun. And then, when it came, a hard, hard rain: not the soft Irish drizzle but a real downpour. My son Rory cavorted in that cooling water for a while, all whoops and giggles. The arrival of a twister sent him into ecstasies: 'it's just like the movies'. But even the rain began to pall in the end.

Rory fled into O'Rourke's, seeking consolation but that took some time. He had just celebrated his twenty-first birthday and his passport said 'DOB 12.7.90'. The sharp-eyed security-man assumed that that meant his first alcoholic drink was still to come: 7 December 2011. He took some persuading that Irish passports give the day, month and year in that order and that Rory had been born on a day sacred to all Orangemen: 12 July 1990. By the time that was settled, Rory was already co-opted by the hard chaws: a real Irishman among 'the Irish'.

Despite this triumph, we wondered whether we would ever feel at home – but soon we did. After a few days on campus, we noticed how often we passed the same, now-familar faces of people who, recognising us too, would say a warm 'hello'. There are indeed no strangers in ND: just friends who haven't yet met. On the third evening, I noticed separate groups of male and female students wending their way to the start-of-academic-year Mass. It was a scene straight out of my own teenage years in Clontarf.

What came to impress me most about the Irish (no inverted, or perverted, commas now) at ND is the energy and enthusiasm with which they embrace their work, play and cultural identity. If only everyone back on the old island had a little more of that self-belief. I sometimes fear that Professors of Irish Studies will reach a point at which they feel that they are expounding a nation on the verge of disappearance. Yet the history of our people is filled with near-death experiences followed by glorious rallies and revivals. We always somehow rise again, a little like the ND footballers.

My spring semester is spent back in my home-place of Dublin, explaining Irish culture to visiting students from ND. At the start, they find it as baffling as I found South Bend – the craziness of Temple Bar on Friday nights, the narrow roads on which cars squeeze past each other at great speed, the tendency of buses to appear in twos or not at all. But eventually they also uncover a world not greatly different from the one they already know - in the rhythms of communal life; in the songs of their grandparents now played on electric guitars in gastro-pubs; above all, in the hand of friendship extended to someone who just ten seconds ago was a stranger.

Bríona Nic Dhiarmada hosts a group of Irish musicians, theatre people and scholars at her home in Tipperary 2012.

From the Heart: Eimear Clowry, Programmes and Communications Manager, Keough Naughton Notre Dame Centre Dublin

It's easy to love what you do when you are surrounded by great people.

On a Saturday morning in September 2008, I first encountered Notre Dame and met my initial group of ND students. We had a lot in common. This being my first day, I felt as much a stranger, as they were to Ireland and each other.

At first we were all a little anxious; shaking hands, sharing names, offering the introductory 'something unusual' about ourselves, nervous laughter getting us through those awkward first few minutes ... and no way of knowing that just a few short months later we would part with lifelong memories, happy members of the ever growing ND Dublin family.

As each group arrives in O'Connell House, a new journey begins. A strange land gradually becomes a home and strangers become friends. Each staff member undertakes that journey anew alongside our fresh batch of students.

Side by side.

We immerse ourselves in Ireland, the music, the food, the language, the people, the landscape, the sun, wind and rain. Together we climb mountains, cross squelchy bogs, fundraise for local charities, cook, celebrate 4 July, sing by candlelight and down thousands of cups of tea and coffee. As we share stories, new ideas, and advice, we learn from each other, most of all about ourselves.

My own journey with O'Connell House has led me to fall in love with Ireland all over again. Experiencing it alongside ND students, seeing it with fresh eyes reminds me how special and often magical a place it is. Through their eyes, I have discovered new ways of experiencing Ireland; reconnecting with its charm, exploring its history, meeting new people. Their genuine enthusiasm for Ireland and its people reinforces my pride in this country.

Our ND students are inspired and invigorated by the footsteps that they trace across the island. For many, this is their first time living abroad, where they learn how to make a grand cup of tea, cook a meal without Mom to supervise, manage their own money and plan their own travel.

Students mature rapidly as they discover their own place in the world, where they come from and more importantly where they want to go in the future. They broaden their understanding of the world they inhabit, they question, they absorb, they stretch themselves and they return home with a deeper understanding of who they are.

For each individual student, and staff member, the journey is different. We learn different things and face different hurdles. But the challenges are easier to overcome and the successes sweeter because we undertake the journey together, side by side.

At the end of each Fall, Spring and Summer session, a shared journey comes to an end. Heartfelt goodbyes leave O'Connell House empty but resonant with laughter, stories and memories.

Soon a new group arrives, awkward, apprehensive but excited for what lies ahead of them. And as we begin a new journey with them, we are reminded that our own journey is never over, that we continue it with the hundreds of alums that take us with them everywhere they go. Looking in the same direction, side by side.

Ireland, the laboratory where God invented rain. Allihies, County Cork.

O'CONNELL HOUSE – HOME OF THE KEOUGH NAUGHTON NOTRE DAME CENTRE, DUBLIN

CHAPTER

O'CONNELL HOUSE

In November 1996, three years after the founding of Irish Studies at Notre Dame, ND football travelled to Dublin, playing Navy at Croke Park. Notre Dame won 54 to 27. The *Irish Times* summarised the game:

> In the end, the giant awoke, grabbed some rolled-up newspaper and gave the pup a good smack on the snout. Notre Dame, who came into the game as favourites but with several questions hanging in the air, put in a solid display to fairly rout Navy in Saturday's Shamrock Classic at Croke Park. The high hopes of the Midshipmen had a long way to fall.

Mark Edwards ran in three touchdowns, while tail back Autry Denson ran in another as Notre Dame focused on a no-frills ground game and Navy had multiple turnovers. Lou Holtz was happy after the game: 'we played well the first half in defence, made some big plays in the second half on defence. I felt our offensive line played very, very well. I thought we played physical, I thought we played aggressive'.

Ten thousand Notre Dame fans made the trip, and the game was instrumental in galvanising new support for ND's Irish connections. Martin Naughton notes: 'My involvement with Notre Dame happened over a football weekend here when ND came to play Navy. Over that life-changing weekend, the idea of establishing an Irish Studies programme, of setting up a campus in Dublin, was being hatched, and many of the visionaries who dreamed that dream are still here to celebrate the tremendous fruits of their efforts'.

Within two years of the game, Notre Dame established a permanent connection to Dublin, setting up the Keough Notre Dame Dublin Study Centre. Initially based in University College Dublin's Newman House, the popular study abroad programme quickly outgrew its confined setting. The University, through the support of Don Keough and Martin Naughton, purchased an elegant Georgian terraced house on Merrion Square – the former home of The

Acquisition of O'Connell House in 2002: Fr. Monk Malloy, CSC (President), Fr. Tim Scully, CSC, Kevin Whelan, Don Keough and Nathan Hatch (Provost).

A detail of the 1790s plasterwork at O'Connell House shows the evocative patina created by age.

Liberator Daniel O'Connell. The Hon. Mr. Justice Adrian Hardiman, Supreme Court of Ireland, noted:

> It is a particular piece of serendipity that Notre Dame has selected this house as its Dublin headquarters. As their Dublin centre, the professors and benefactors found a building not merely adequate and distinguished, but one which is itself a piece of Irish history.

GEORGIAN DUBLIN AND MERRION SQUARE

Daniel O'Connell lived most of his life at 58 Merrion Square, a late eighteenth-century building located in the most impressive set-piece of the Georgian city. Merrion Square was laid out from 1762 onwards, under the auspices of the Fitzwilliam estate, as Dublin expanded rapidly to become 'the second city' of the British Empire. The German traveller J. G. Kohl described Merrion Square in 1843 as 'the most beautiful one in the British Empire'. The neo-classical style championed proportion in architecture as being equivalent to harmony in music, seeking to set eternal verities in stone. The characteristic Georgian architecture exemplified restrained deployment of proportion and balance; mathematical ratios determined the height of a window in relation to its width, or the shape of a room as a double cube.

Merrion Square, modelled on Parisian and London prototypes, was planned with a high degree of architectural specification, designed to maintain the coherence of the streetscape. Barbara Verschoyle was responsible for completion of this elegant project, rendering Merrion Square unique as an enlightenment set-piece largely created by a woman. Although the square was actually constructed by speculative builders with limited capital who could only finance a few buildings at a time, uniformity was achieved under her watchful eye by imposing consistency of building materials, fenestration, and equal street frontages.

Maurice Craig describes the Dublin streetscape as possessing 'a cliff-like reticence, relieved by the warmth of the brick, lightened by the breadth of the streets'. The exterior sobriety is balanced by Dublin's exuberant love affair with gaudy door colours. The uniform terrace of houses first appeared in London in 1717 at Old Burlington Street and quickly spread to Dublin. The terrace deployed a standard vocabulary to ensure that individual houses blended seamlessly into the architectural whole: a plain brick facade, a string course, a crowning cornice, moulded architraves and door cases, sash windows, cast-iron balconies, a top-lit oculus, fine fanlights, Venetian windows around the door. Windows were set back to leave the woodwork less exposed to fire risk. Glazing bars were necessary because glass was expensive and sheet glass unobtainable until after 1825.

This 1840s painting of O'Connell in its elaborate gilded frame was restored to O'Connell House in 2012. Below it is Lynn Kramer's head of Seamus Heaney – and a sod of turf from Toner's Bog, Bellaghy.

of the dark, to reconnoitre the interior, you will see a tall, able-bodied man standing at a desk, and immersed in solitary occupation. No sooner can the eye take in the other furniture of the apartment, the bookcases clogged with tomes in reams of manuscript in oblong folds and begirt with crimson tape, than it becomes evident that he is unquestionably a barrister, but, apparently, of that homely, chamber-keeping, plodding cast, who labour hard to make up by assiduity what they want in wit ... Should you happen to stroll down to the hall of the Four Courts, you will not be a little surprised to find the object of your pity miraculously transformed from the severe recluse of the morning into one of the most bustling, important, and joyous personages in that busy scene.

Movita, painted by Seán Keating

O'Connell's political career was orchestrated from Merrion Square, where he often addressed the crowd from the first-floor balcony. Mary Francis Cusack described the scene after his release from prison in 1844. 'All through the long route from O'Connell's house in Merrion Square to the prison, thousands had assembled and kept perfect order. Such a scene was never witnessed in Dublin. There was not a single policeman seen or needed in all that vast multitude. When O'Connell reached his house in Merrion Square, he addressed the people'.

The family lived happily here until the death of the Liberator in 1847. O'Connell sacrificed his earning potential as a lawyer to serve his people. His debt-beleaguered family had to sell off the furniture in September 1847, followed by the library in 1849, and the house itself in 1853, breaking the O'Connell connection. A placque on the external wall now marks the historic character of the house where The Liberator lived.

LATER RESIDENTS

O'Connell House now passed into professional (mainly medical) hands until 1935, with gynaecologists and obstetricians using it as consulting rooms for Holles Street Maternity Hospital on the other side of Merrion Square. It was used for business purposes from 1936 onwards, and also as a residence. Its most flamboyant residents were 'Gorgeous' Jack Doyle (1913-1978) and his glamorous Mexican film-star wife Movita. Maria 'Movita' Castaneda (born in 1917) was best known for playing exotic women/singers, such as in *Flying Down to Rio* (1933) and *Mutiny on the Bounty* (1935).

Doyle, a boxer, singer, hell-raiser, alcoholic, playboy and celebrity, was a six foot three inch Irishman with a gargantuan appetite for life. In 1933, he attracted 60,000 to London's White City to see him fight. By the age of thirty, he had already made and squandered a fortune on 'slow horses and fast women' (in his own words), operating under his mantra: 'A generous man never went to hell'. In his heyday, he was a major celebrity. He and Movita – the Mexican Evita – comprised a power couple as popular as Olivier and Leigh, or Burton

'Chin-angles or how the poets passed each other'. An Isa Macnie cartoon celebrates a famous incident concerning writers, and Merrion Square neighbours, Yeats and George Russell. Yeats characteristically strode around with his nose in the air; the introspective Russell kept his eyes downcast. Here they pass unheedingly in the street.

and Taylor. His addictive personality eventually derailed Jack Doyle, who became a faded celebrity, scratching a living as an all-in wrestler before sinking deep into alcoholism, and dying as a down-and-out in London. Movita divorced him in the 1940s, returned to Hollywood, and married Marlon Brando.

Other celebrated residents of Merrion Square include William Butler Yeats, Oscar Wilde, the Gothic novelist Joseph Sheridan Le Fanu, the poet and mystic George Russell (AE), Irish-language scholar Whitley Stokes, Nobel prize winner Erwin Schrodinger, and Irish-American sculptor Andrew O'Connor.

NOTRE DAME ACQUIRES O'CONNELL HOUSE

O'Connell House was purchased by the University of Notre Dame in May 2002. The acquisition allowed the University's Dublin operations much needed space to expand, as well as a storied location for international studies. We believe the property to be the oldest owned by the University – either on campus and overseas. The prime mover in this process was Fr. Tim Scully, CSC, then Executive Vice-President at Notre Dame. Ordained a Holy Cross priest in 1981, he earned his doctoral degree in Political Science from Berkeley, before becoming a Professor of Political Science at Notre Dame.

Liam Cosgrave, former Taoiseach, with Kevin Whelan and Fr. Sean McGraw, CSC.

Actors Stephen Rea and Sineád Cusack.

Kerry Footballer Darragh Ó Sé, with Lisa Caulfield and Kevin Whelan.

Actor Eamon Morrissey with Ashley Fox, 2012.

Seamus Heaney, c. 1977, by the celebrated English photographer Jane Bown.

Seamus Heaney signs a volume for Provost Tom Burish in the front Square TCD, after Notre Dame conferred an Honorary Degree on him in 2008.

Fr. Scully also founded Notre Dame's Alliance for Catholic Education in 1994, and he is currently Director of Institute for Educational Initiatives.

THE HEANEY COLLECTION AT O'CONNELL HOUSE

Seamus Heaney, Nobel Laureate in 1995, is widely regarded as the most significant living poet in the world. The Heaney Collection at the Keough Naughton Notre Dame Centre consists of over 200 signed volumes, comprising the first editions of every book or pamphlet that Mr. Heaney has published. The collection includes many of the holy grails of Heaney collecting. The earliest volume is *Eleven Poems*, his first slim volume published in a tiny edition in Belfast in 1965. Other highlights include *A Lough Neagh Sequence* (1969), *Stations* (1975), *After Summer* (1978), *Hedge School* (1979), and *Clearances*

(1986). These and many other volumes rarely surface on the antiquarian market, and are of legendary scarcity.

The collection was assembled painstakingly by Ian Steepe, Dublin schoolteacher and bibliophile, over a period of five decades. Because he stored the books in a bank vault, they are in mint condition. This collection gives Notre Dame a world-class research collection, tracking in exhaustive detail the evolution of this great poet. O'Connell House has also added many fine images of Heaney, including rare photographs by Jane Bown and Sally Soames, prints by Louis le Brocquy and Neil Shawcross, and a sculpted head by American sculptor Lynn Kramer.

Seamus Deane, the inaugurator of the Irish Studies programme at Notre Dame in 1993, was Heaney's classmate in Derry and in Queens University Belfast, and they subsequently worked together closely in the Field Day Theatre Company. Heaney has made several visits to Notre Dame (including public readings in 1995 and 2003), featured frequently at ND's annual Irish Seminar in Dublin since 1999, and often visits O'Connell House. Seamus Heaney was awarded an honorary doctorate by the university in 2008. Heaney dedicated his reading of the poem *Miracle:*

> to Don and Mickie Keough and to Martin and Carmel Naughton – people who are constant reminders of the truth of Ralph Waldo Emerson's claim that 'institutions are the lengthened shadows of individuals'; two sets of people who are utterly essential to the action, who stand quietly aside like the friends - two miracles of disinterested giving, of utter philanthropy.

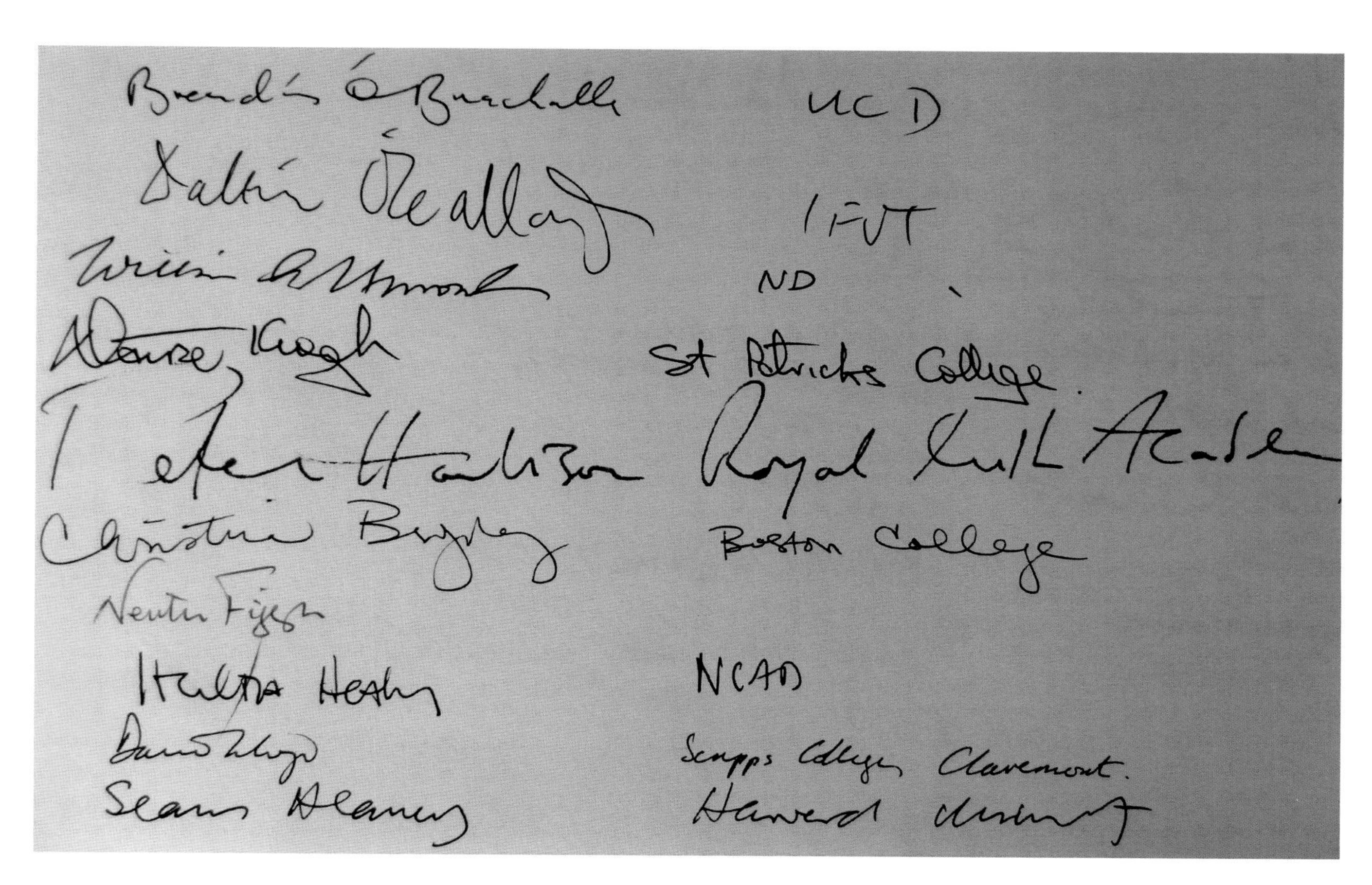

O'Connell House hosts many public events. Among the attendance on this occasion were Seamus Heaney, Breandán Ó Buachalla, the archaeologist Peter Harbison, Daire Keogh, President of St. Patrick's College, and the Irish Studies scholar David Lloyd.

The Yellow Bittern

Seamus Heaney

Yellow bittern, there you are now,
Skin and bone on the frozen shore.
It wasn't hunger but thirst for a mouthful
That left you foundered and me heartsore.
What odds is it now about Troy's destruction
With you on the flagstones upside down,
Who never injured or hurt a creature
And preferred bog-water to any wine?

Bittern, bittern, your end was awful,
Your perished skull there on the road,
You that would call me every morning
With your gargler's song as you guzzled mud!
And that's what's ahead of your brother Cathal
(You know what they say about me and the stuff)
But they've got it wrong and the truth is simple -
A drop would have saved the croaker's life.

I am saddened, bittern, and broken-hearted
To find you in scrags in the rushy tufts,
And the big rats scampering down the ratpaths
To wake your carcass and have their fun.
If you could have got word to me in time, bird,
That you were in trouble and craved a sup,
I'd have struck the fetters off those lough waters
And wet your thrapple with the blow I struck.

Your common birds do not concern me,
The blackbird, say, or the thrush or crane,
But the yellow bittern, my heartsome namesake
With my looks and locks, he's the one I mourn.
Constantly he was drinking, drinking,
And by all accounts I've a name for it too,
But every drop I get I'll sink it
For fear I might get my end from the drouth.

The woman I love says to give it up now
Or else I'll go to an early grave,
But I say no and keep resisting
For taking drink's what prolongs your days.
You saw for yourselves a while ago
What happened the bird when its throat went dry;
So my friends and neighbours, let it flow:
You'll be stood no rounds in eternity.

A translation of *An Bonnán Buí*
by Cathal Mac Giolla Ghunna (c. 1680-1756)

Keough Naughton
Notre Dame Centre

invites you to a

Private
Poetry Reading

by

Seamus Heaney

at

7pm Thursday 17 June

Reception 6pm

O'Connell House

58 Merrion Square
Dublin 2

Published by the Keough-Notre Dame Centre, Dublin to celebrate the fourth IRISH SEMINAR, July 2002. Design by Caroline Moloney. Limited edition of 50 of which this is no. [41]

The Yellow Bittern: An Invitation Issued by the Keough Naughton Notre Dame Centre Dublin to a Heaney reading in 2010.

PANGUR BÁN

Messe ocus Pangur bán,
Cechtar nacthar fria ṡaindán:
  Bith a menmasam fri seilgg,
  Mu menma céin im ṡaincheirdd.

Caraimse fos, ferr cach clú,
Oc mu lebrān, lēir ingnu;
  Ni foirmtech frimm Pangur bán:
  Caraid cesin a macdan.

Ō ru biam, scél cen scís,
Innar tegdais, ar n-ōendís,
  Tāithiunn, dīchrīchide clius,
  Nī fris tarddam ar n-áthius.

Gnáth, hūaraib, ar gressaib gal
glenaid luch inna línsam;
  os mé, du-fuit im lín chéin
  dliged ndoraid cu ndronchéill.

Fūachaidsem fri frega fál
A rosc, a nglése comlán;
  Fūaichimm chēin fri fēgi fis,
  mu rosc rēil, cesu imdis.

Fāelidsem cu ndēne dul
Hi nglen luch inna gērchrub;
  Hi tucu cheist ndoraid ndil
  Os me chene am fāelid.

Cia beimmi a-min nach ré
Nī derban cách a chēle:
  Maith la cechtar nár a dán;
  Subaigthius a oénurán.

Hē feisin as choimsid dáu
In muid du-ngní cach ōenláu;
  Du thubairt doraid du glé
  For mu mud cēin am messe.

Pangur Bán and I at work
Adepts, equals, cats and clerk:
  His whole instinct is to hunt,
  Mine to free the meaning pent.

More than loud acclaim, I love
Books, silence, thought, my alcove.
  Happy for me, Pangur Bán
  Child-plays round some mouse's den.

Truth to tell, just being here,
Housed alone, housed together,
  Adds up to its own reward:
  Concentration, stealthy art.

Next thing an unwary mouse
Bares his flank: Pangur pounces.
  Next thing lines that held and held
  Meaning back begin to yield.

All the while, his round bright eye
Fixes on the wall, while I
  Exercise my weaker gaze
  On the sharply argued page.

With his unsheathed, perfect nails
Pangur springs, exults and kills.
  When the longed-for, difficult
  Answers come, I too exult.

So it goes. To each his own.
No vying. No vexation.
  Taking pleasure, taking pains,
  Kindred spirits, veterans.

Day and night, soft purr, soft pad,
Pangur Bán has learned his trade.
  Day and night, my own hard work
  Solves the cruxes, makes a mark.

Translated from an anonymous ninth-century Irish poem by

Seamus Heaney

Design: Caroline Moloney & Kevin Whelan

Pangur Bán: Issued by the Keough Naughton Notre Dame Centre Dublin to mark Seamus Heaney's visit to Stackallan House, 2006.

Learning through the soles of your feet.
In Connemara Spring 2012.

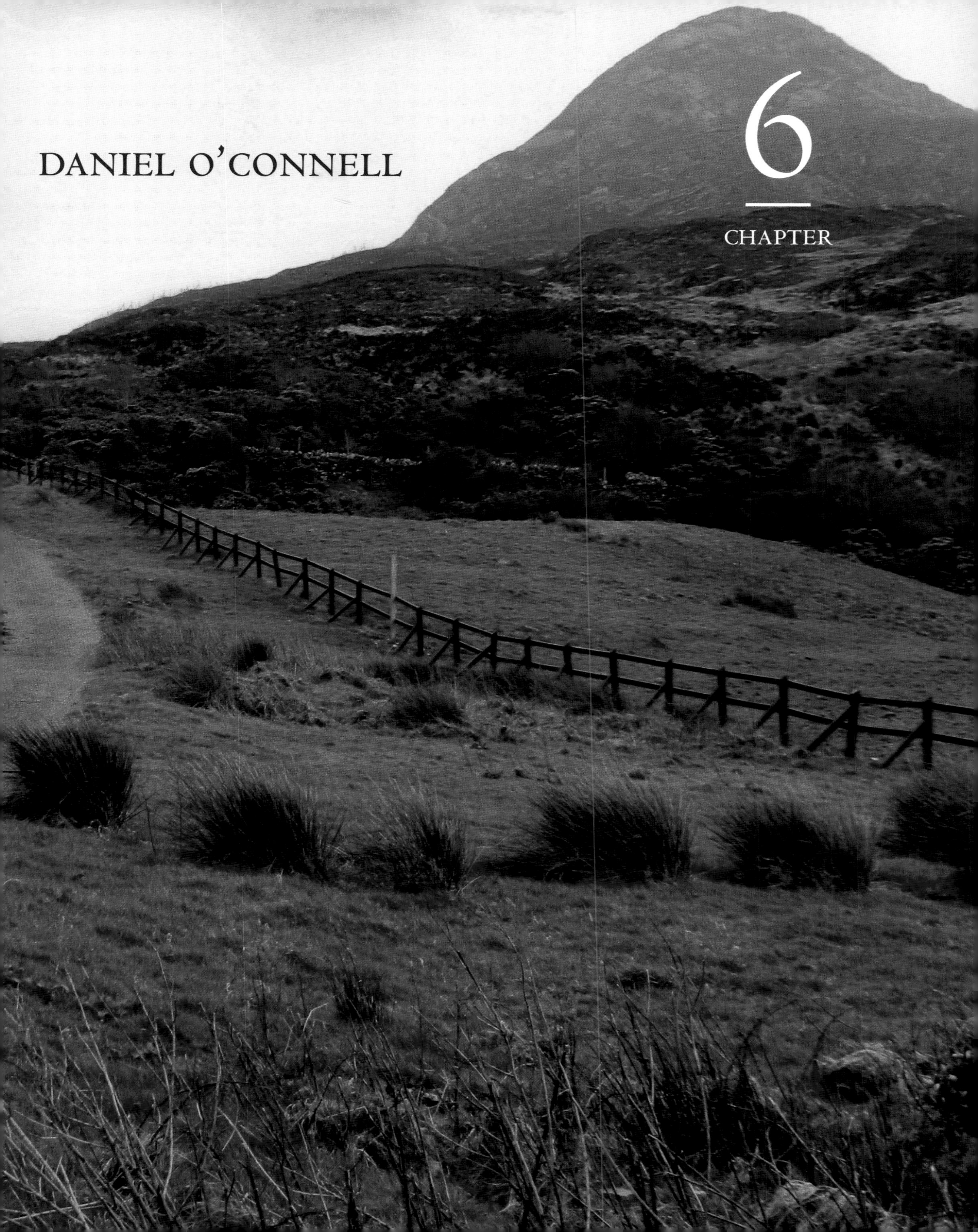

6

CHAPTER

DANIEL O'CONNELL

Daniel O'Connell in 1842 (from the fashionable Paris magazine, *Le Charivari*).

DANIEL O'CONNELL

Daniel O'Connell gloried in being born during the American Revolution:

> Be it known to all whom it may concern that I was born on the 6th August 1775, the very year in which the stupid obstinacy of British oppression forced the reluctant people of America to seek for security in arms, and to commence that bloody struggle for national independence which has been in its results beneficial to England while it has shed Glory and conferred Liberty pure and sublime on America.

O'Connell was reared in an Irish-speaking environment in County Kerry, where the ancestral home was at Derrynane. Throughout his life, O'Connell retained the instinctive feel of a populist politician for ordinary people – most importantly for what they felt rather than what they said – a legacy of his childhood immersion in their interior life. Fostered by a tenant for four years and educated in a hedge school, he grew up within the expansive tradition of hospitality enjoyed by the Kerry middleman families of the O'Connell's social standing. He was immersed in a cultural world of duelling, hurling, hunting, and smuggling. O'Connell had extensive and intimate Wild Geese connections and his life was lived within the overlapping circles of kinship, 'an eternal relay of cousins'.

Never a great writer, he communicated his politics through oratory, and he was a master at tailoring his message to suit his audience. His wit, vituperative humour and showmanship gave him enormous command when speaking, never more so than when the crowd was large; O'Connell fed off his audiences as they fed off him. He was constantly reinventing himself, his campaigns and his tactics, a protean figure of endless energy and insatiable combativeness. He also carefully cultivated his self-image. A master of political theatre, he blended oratorical flamboyance with meticulous organisation, imposing his massive personality on every aspect of a national movement.

His fatal duel with the ultra-Protestant John D'Esterre on 1 February 1815 confirmed his defense of national honour, conferring the mantle of protector of the Irish Catholics on him. O'Connell comported himself as the personal embodiment of his country: as he put it in 1831, 'he was the man of the people (an Irish language poem uses the epithet 'Duine na daoine') – that they look'd up to him and that no feelings of a publick or private nature should ever operate to disappoint their just dependence on him'. No one so saturated the Irish popular imagination. More folklore survives on him than on any other single individual in Irish history. In Joyce's phrase, 'a whole people sheltered within his voice'.

O'Connell's religious formation evolved from his Kerry childhood through his Counter-Reformation Catholic education in France, then his sceptical Deist days influenced by Paine, Godwin and Voltaire, and culminating in his repaired relationship with the Church. Under his wife Mary's persistent prodding, O'Connell conscientiously received the sacraments and followed Church doctrine. O'Connell believed that there was no incompatibility between his religious and his political ideas. He was able to create a novel blend of Catholicism and radicalism, two concepts hitherto considered incompatible. Although O'Connell maintained a strong sense

Fr. Sean McGraw, CSC, and Kevin Whelan at Derrynane House, County Kerry, ancestral O'Connell home.

of Catholic identity and acknowledged papal authority in the areas of faith and doctrine, he deplored the temporal power and possessions of the Church. Throughout O'Connell's political career, he fought for freedom of religious practice and belief for all, not just Catholics, and the absolute separation of Church and State. O'Connell responded to his critics that 'If I did not believe that the Catholic religion could compete upon equal and free terms with any other religion, I would not continue a Catholic for a minute'.

O'Connell consistently retained a belief in the power of the law to effect social and political change. The failure to incorporate Catholics fully into the new United Kingdom in 1801 convinced them that there was a close link between their political impotence and their legal isolation. O'Connell absolutely shared this conviction, informed by his daily experiences in Irish courts. He was to be the ultimate beneficiary of this politicisation of the law in the eyes of Irish Catholics. It was no accident that his rise to political dominance within his own community followed his spectacularly successful legal career, nor that his popular persona was rooted in his role as 'An Cunsailéir', endlessly running rhetorical rings around British law.

A common thread throughout O'Connell's long career was his consistent opposition to the use of violence. O'Connell used the term 'bloodless revolution' to describe his own achievement in winning Catholic Emancipation. His capacity to harness what he called the 'moral force' of mass non-violent action became his lasting contribution to the emerging Ireland. O'Connell's innovation was to actualise the latent potential of superior Catholic numbers. The first detailed religious census in 1834 turned in Catholics at 81% of the total population of Ireland.

The Catholic Association, founded by O'Connell in 1823, flexed this newly conditioned political muscle. The democratic penny-a-month membership, co-option of priests, the widespread distribution of the *Catholic Register*, and the careful cultivation of a coterie of politically astute organisers created an unprecedented mobilisation of Irish Catholics. The Catholic Association eventually decided to challenge landlord control of this Catholic vote. The campaign's spearhead would be the structures and personnel of the institutional church – the sole national institution available, sympathetic and responsive to Irish Catholic needs.

The 1826 general election provided an opportunity to bring this newly-honed weapon to bear on O'Connell's constant target – the Irish Protestant gentry and their unearned constitutional privileges. O'Connell stood a liberal Protestant as a 'Catholic' candidate in Waterford. His election achieved a symbolic victory of stunning proportions for the Catholics. The transition effectively marked the end of the road for the Irish landed gentry as the dominant player in Irish politics. O'Connell conducted a further audacious coup in 1828 when he personally won the Clare by-election. These sweeping victories were irresistible demonstrations of political momentum. The Catholic Emancipation Act of 1829 inevitably followed. O'Connell was instantly dubbed 'The Liberator' by his grateful Irish supporters.

The ineffectual aristocratic Catholic leader Lord Fingall noted on his deathbed in 1836: 'We never understood that we had a nation behind us. O'Connell alone comprehended that properly and he used his knowledge fitly. It was by him the gates of the constitution were broken open for us: we owe everything to his rough work'. The German Prince Puckler Muskau was impressed:

> Daniel O'Connell is no common man, though he is a man of the people. His power in Ireland is so great at this moment he could single handedly raise the banner of revolt from one end of the island to the other, if he were not much too clear-sighted and much too sure of his success by far less dangerous means. By legal, openly publicised methods, cleverly using the moment and mood of the nation, he has created this power over the people which, without army or weapons, is yet like that of a king.

O'Connell insisted on the necessity for Catholics to be fully incorporated on equal terms within the public sphere of post-emancipation Ireland. One of the most galling aspects of the Penal Laws was that they consigned Catholics – the majority of the population – to a permanent status as non-citizens. After Catholic Emancipation, O'Connell led Catholics in a determined campaign to reclaim that public space: hence it was essential for O'Connell to make the Catholic presence felt. His 'Monster Meetings', rallies, parades and processions around the Dublin streets all staked out the public space as open to Catholics, unhindered by the previous collusion between the state and the gentry to keep them invisible and marginalised. He also sought to strengthen Irish masculinity

O'Connell was held in huge regard in Dublin. Here he speaks, in 1844, to an enthusiastic crowd from the balcony of O'Connell House.

O'CONNELL AT THE BALCONY, IN MERRION-SQUARE, DUBLIN.

NATION.

DUBLIN, SATURDAY, SEPTEMBER 20, 1845. PRICE 6D.

Just published, price 1s. 6d.,
YNE, 4 Capel-street, Printer and Bookseller to
. of St. Patrick, Maynooth, and Publisher to
ian Catholic Bishops of Ireland,
RIES of PRACTICAL MEDITATIONS
ON THE
OBLIGATIONS AND VIRTUES
OF
TIAN AND RELIGIOUS PERFECTION.
to all Classes of the Christian and Catholic
Community.

VESTMENTS, GOLD AND SILVER LACE.

THEOLOGICAL AND RELIGIOUS BOOKS, Italian and French Engravings, Porcelain Vases, Fonts and Statues, Artificial Flowers, Ivory and Bronze Crucifixes, Rosary Beads and Medals; English, French, and Italian Prayer Books, bound in Ivory, Tortoiseshell, and Morocco, with illuminated Prints and Clasps; Stations of the Cross in Statuary, Coloured and Plain Engravings, Altar Pieces of various sizes, Rich Altar Candlesticks,

AMERICAN SLAVERY.

FREDERICK DOUGLAS, recently a Slave in the United States, intends to deliver ANOTHER LECTURE, in the MUSIC-HALL, Lower Abbey-street, on TUESDAY Evening next, 23d instant, at Eight o'clock.
Doors to be open at Half-past Seven o'clock.
Admission, by tickets, to be had at the door.
Promenade—Fourpence. Gallery—Twopence.

DUBLIN CONSUMERS' GAS COMPANY.

An advertisement in *The Nation* for Douglass's Dublin lecture, 20 September 1845.

Known as 'the Black O'Connell', Frederick Douglass modelled his oratorical style on the Irishman.

In 2011, the descendants of Douglass paid a visit to O'Connell House. Nettie Washington Douglass, great-great-granddaughter of Frederick Douglass, and her son Kenneth Morris.

by encouraging the Irish to stand tall in place of 'the subdued demeanour and almost crouching walk' that he associated with their penal subjugation. He called the Irish people 'crawling slaves' in 1839.

O'Connell's own stance on slavery was consistent. He called for 'speedy, immediate abolition' in 1831 and attacked the white republic and American hypocrisy, remaining principled on this issue even when it hurt him with his Irish-American constituency. His vehemence – 'we do not want blood-stained money' – split American Repeal societies. In his opinion, shared oppression should have nurtured a political affinity between Irish Catholics and African-Americans, a principled internationalism, and he was puzzled as to how the Irish embraced 'cruelty' in America by supporting the slavery cause. O'Connell personally declined to set foot in the USA while it remained a slave society. He refused to set limits to his principles, and he never allowed his broad ethical vision to be narrowed by Irish concerns. In 1830, he observed: 'Ireland and Irishmen should be foremost in seeking to effect the emancipation of mankind'. In 1845, he stressed that 'My sympathy with distress is not confined within the narrow bounds of my own green island – it extends itself to every corner of the earth'.

His efforts were recognised within America. In 1833, the African-American Church in New York held a meeting honouring O'Connell: 'the uncompromising advocate of universal emancipation, the friend of oppressed Africans and their descendants and the unadulterated rights of man'. He was also visited in Dublin in 1845 by his great admirer Frederick Douglass.

Just as they reclaimed public space, Catholics also sought access to the public sphere – the domain of civil society, mediated by print culture. O'Connell's ability to orchestrate a national campaign depended on the second print revolution that gathered momentum in the 1820s. O'Connell was quick to realise the potential of the print media to foster national opinion and hence mobilise campaigns. O'Connell's revolution was the democratisation of Irish politics, an achievement which soon generated spillover effects in Britain. In this sense, the long eighteenth century lasted from 1690 to 1829 in Irish politics and it was O'Connell who terminated it. His victory in forcing the British state to shed its sectarian character was followed by the Great Reform Act of 1832 that marked the British transition from a regressive *ancien regime* to a modern parliamentary democracy.

O'Connell's long dominance of nationalist politics was finally challenged in the 1840s though the growing disenchantment of the group coalescing around the *Nation* newspaper (established 1842) which was eventually to be called Young Ireland. They formed part of a common European trend: there were other young movements across Europe, notably in Italy, Switzerland, Austria, Greece and Bohemia. The philosophical underpinnings of Irish nationalism shifted dramatically in the second half of the nineteenth century. O'Connell's political philosophy – essentially late enlightened liberalism – was eclipsed with the spread of Romanticism. This philosophical difference was the intellectual basis of O'Connell's split with Young Ireland in the 1840s. Within Irish nationalism, the emphasis on cultural nationality found little to admire in the pragmatic O'Connellite approach.

O'Connell's significance should always be understood within the larger European context. He offered a role model for other European Catholic activists, because he invented an authentic relationship between tradition and modernity, and between Catholicism and democracy, salvaging positive aspects of the enlightenment without succumbing to its irreligion. This is why O'Connell proved so inspiring to the European Catholic liberals, who sought to advance Catholicism beyond an automatic association with social conservatism, the monarch and a return to the *ancien regime*. O'Connell proved that it was possible to reconcile the hierarchical world of Catholic obedience with secular democratic values of individual autonomy and equality. Other Catholic nationalist movements emerged across Europe in the first half of the nineteenth century. Poland and Belgium, closely observing the Irish example, developed a similar blend of persecuted national traditions and Catholicism, which jettisoned Enlightenment irreligion and anti-clericalism, while retaining its democratic principles.

While O'Connell is conventionally seen as a commanding figure in Irish politics, he was also arguably the most influential Catholic activist in nineteenth-century European politics. He fused Catholicism with enlightened thinking in a potent combination that fascinated continental Catholics. Alexis de Tocqueville visited Ireland in 1835 to explore at first hand the O'Connell phenomenon of a mass-based Catholic democratic movement. In that sense, O'Connell can legitimately be claimed as an early progenitor of the European Christian Democratic tradition.

Martin Naughton, Mary and Martin McAleese, and Don Keough at the dedication of O'Connell House, 2004.

Speech by President Mary McAleese, opening of O'Connell House, 16 October 2004

Tá an-athás orm bheith anseo i bhur measc innu. Go raibh míle maith agaibh as ucht bhur bhfáilte caoin. Good afternoon, everybody. May I begin by congratulating the University of Notre Dame on the superb job of restoration we see around us, and by thanking the Keough and Naughton families for their generous assistance in making the restoration possible. The dedication of this house is a fitting and hugely symbolic act that draws to a close the refurbishment of a building intimately associated with The Liberator. It occurs on the anniversary of the re-opening, fifty-five years ago today, of the little chapel at O'Connell's home in Kerry, Derrynane House.

Ceremonies such as these remind us of O'Connell's greatness even as they point to the degree to which his name has been unfairly neglected. Not that it was ever obscure, but it is an odd thing that although O'Connell's memory is preserved in the names of the streets throughout Ireland, it seemed at times as if he would become the forgotten hero of Ireland's past.

Perhaps we should blame W. B. Yeats. When Yeats described the death of 'romantic Ireland', he named the heroes who should be remembered and asked of more mundane times, was it

> For this Edward Fitzgerald died,
> And Robert Emmet and Wolfe Tone,
> All that delirium of the brave?

In that pantheon of freedom, O'Connell appeared as a pale figure by comparison with his more colourful fellow patriots. Perhaps O'Connell was not romantic enough or militant enough for a world held in thrall by the shallow excitement and glamour of violence. But whatever the reason, it does not really explain the degree to which the legacy of O'Connell does not receive the popular acclaim it deserves.

We rightly honour the patriots of our past, shapers of our history and our mind maps of that history. Throughout generations of appalling suffering they led rebellions of the poor and dispossessed, mostly it has to be said without immediate success. O'Connell's campaigns were very different. Non-violent in nature but nonetheless persuasive and popular, his hard work produced results. Catholic Emancipation was an immense achievement. And perhaps the Repeal of the Union might have been achieved if the collapse of his health and the Famine following shortly thereafter had not derailed his hopes. So great was the force of his argument that even some Unionists applied to join the Repeal movement.

He was educated abroad, because it was not possible in those days for a Catholic to graduate from Dublin University. He put his education to very good use by becoming the unparalleled political and legal advocate of his age. His eloquence was based on an absolute command of detail and profound grasp of the issues he was addressing. He could appeal to the heads and hearts of very different people in a direct way. He was an Irish speaking countryman to his countrymen, he was the sophisticated European in the salons of the powerful. After Emancipation, he dominated the British Parliament by the force of his oratory and the precise forensic analysis of his opponents' views.

O'Connell's campaign against the Penal Laws was a major intellectual as well as a major political breakthrough. After the disastrous failure of the French Revolution, it seemed that the struggle for democracy was effectively thrown into reverse. With the turmoil of the Napoleonic Wars still vivid in the memories of most people, O'Connell devised a new politics which demonstrated that the goals which had inspired the best of the Revolution could be pursued without descending into the pit of violent oppression which was produced by that Revolution at its worst.

He was a fervent and life-long opponent of political violence and the use of force. Instead of organising a revolt, O'Connell took largely uneducated country people and built them into a great mass political organisation. A political organisation with extraordinary moral courage and determination. A political force which achieved its goals without recourse to the violence which had been the hallmark of the Irish resistance up until then.

Daniel O'Connell hated injustice. His politics were rooted in the egalitarian and libertarian principles of the new American republic, which he had absorbed and from which he never faltered. His intellectual achievement was to marry those principles to the parliamentary traditions of Europe. In that achievement, he showed Ireland, Europe, and the world, that the eighteenth-century pillars upon which the struggle for liberty had been built had not been lost forever in the tidal wave which swept the *Ancien regime* back into power.

The principles of Liberty, Equality and Fraternity, had been the product of an enlightened vanguard of thinkers who illuminate our political discourse to this day. The enterprise, which began as an attempt to impose freedom from above, quickly turned into the Terror, a pattern to be repeated, not as a farce but as a tragedy, in the twentieth century.

The genius of O'Connell was to create a peaceful but forceful campaign for liberty from the bottom up. His mass movement for Catholic Emancipation had the support of members of every class of society. The penny rent was an ingenious system for financing the movement, but it also copper fastened the common commitment to shared goals in the first mass political movement, probably, in the world.

In other words, O'Connell had invented, and wielded to great effect, the first modern political party. Today, as then, the political party system can be untidy and diffuse, but it makes room for a broad sweep of opinion and gives everybody a platform and a say in the decisions which affect them. And in large measure we owe it to O'Connell.

We forget, to our own loss, that O'Connell was a giant of a figure who bestrode the platform of European politics of his day. But O'Connell's vision extended well beyond his owns shores: he promoted justice on the basis of principle, and was a powerful advocate of, for example, the end of the slave trade and civil rights for European Jews.

Today, for all the statues in his memory and the streets named in his honour, his greatest monument is the foundation he laid a long time ago for the peace process of today and the Good Friday Agreement. His influence in moulding the moderate, non-violent and democratic political tradition has been, over time, both the dominant and the most valuable strand of our national public life. He would certainly recognise, as familiar and valued principles, the commitment to resolving our differences through democratic process and peaceful means; a dedication to the promotion of partnership and equality; a promise to vindicate and protect the human rights of all members of all communities on the island of Ireland. The Good Friday Agreement has not yet reached final fulfilment. Suspicion and old vanities still impede its complete implementation, though the elements, including human rights, continue to make slow, but real, progress.

The continuing support and encouragement of the international community, and of Ireland's many friends overseas, is of tremendous encouragement to us. Nowhere is this truer than in the United States. Successive Presidents and leading figures from both parties in the Congress and at state level, have played a crucial role in developing and sustaining the peace process. The Irish-American community has displayed unfaltering understanding and commitment.

As we stand on the eve of a new Ireland and reflect on the past, I am confident that O'Connell's vision of peace and justice will prevail, just as I am confident that Ireland is on a path to completing the work of creating a fully inclusive egalitarian Ireland begun by O' Connell and coming into our grasp in this blessed of generations. I have no doubt too that O'Connell would view today's successful, confident Ireland with a deep sense of pride, hope and personal vindication. Could this be the very generation he worked for, the first to know true peace, widespread prosperity and respectful partnership between Ireland's different strands? That we are this close is thanks to him, the man once dubbed 'Ireland's uncrowned monarch', a title he would surely have rejected though he might have taken a different view had he been more accurately called Ireland's 'un-inaugurated President'.

Our thanks to those who have once again brought his memory, his legacy before us to inspire and encourage us to complete the journey he started. Go raibh maith agaibh go léir.

O'Connell parade in Dublin in 1835. It is about to pass the spot where his monument now stands on O'Connell Street.

O'Connell's funeral passes his family home in 1847.

Achill Island Spring 2011.

NOTRE DAME'S DUBLIN PROGRAMMES

7

CHAPTER

NOTRE DAME'S DUBLIN PROGRAMMES

UNDERGRADUATE PROGRAMME

Founded in 1998, the undergraduate study abroad programme at the Keough Naughton Centre has seen 1,005 students pass through its doors by 2012. One of Notre Dame's most competitive programmes, the Dublin Centre welcomes students from all undergraduate disciplines. While in Dublin, students study at the top two Irish universities, Trinity College Dublin (TCD) and University College Dublin (UCD), and there are also specialist options in the National College of Art and Design and the Royal Irish Academy of Music. A unique hybrid, the Dublin programme replicates elements of an immersed programme, allowing students to plunge independently into Irish life in Irish universities and culture, while still retaining the level of student support typical of Notre Dame.

To an ND sophomore, the idea of studying abroad for all or part of junior year can seem unimaginable. Most have finally determined the quickest route from their dorm to DeBartolo Hall, many have just embarked on the official programme of study in their newly declared major, others have established a close-knit group of friends, and few have the motivation to find their way to Carroll Hall, let alone a foreign country.

With at least a decade of rigorous academic and extra-curricular work behind them in the hopes of receiving that coveted acceptance letter, one might think that the likelihood of ND students choosing to leave their beautiful campus is less than the chances of a snow-free South Bend winter. Yet, with over half of ND students going overseas during their undergraduate career, ND continually ranks among the nation's top twenty universities for the highest percentage of students enrolled in study abroad.

With 41 programmes on offer, Notre Dame offers an array of unique opportunities in twenty countries, each with its unique history, culture, language, and landscape. Since its inception in 1998, however, the Dublin programme has remained a perennial favourite, and applicants count themselves lucky to get an acceptance letter, the golden ticket that allows them to behold Ireland's green patchwork quilt with their very own eyes.

The beginning of their adventure: students in Dublin Airport, Spring 2008.

While some Doyles, Ryans and O'Neills apply to Dublin to reconnect with distant relatives and to learn about their heritage, many others seek the multiple opportunities that Dublin and Ireland have to offer. At ND's partner institutions, TCD and UCD, students can study at highly ranked and well-known institutions, in subjects that they might not be able to explore at home. The Quinn School of Business at UCD allows undergrads to study the international economy in one of the most globalised countries in the world. The Schools of History, English, and Archaeology at TCD and UCD allow students to learn about major events in Irish and world history, mere miles from the Hill of Tara, Dublin Castle and Kilmainham Gaol. Students are on the doorstep of Europe as well, allowing them to learn about a topic in class, and then see it in reality. Archaeology students go on digs, a practical element that is key to their education. In recent years, ND students have also enrolled at the National College of Art and Design and the Royal Irish Academy of Music, learning from excellent scholars in their fields, working with a highly international student body, and winning key design and performance competitions.

The academic possibilities are not limited to those presented by their host institutions. ND students have also ready access to noted scholars in literature, history, film, theology, philosophy, and the Irish language at O'Connell House, Notre Dame's Dublin Centre. World-renowned faculty such as Declan Kiberd, Seamus Deane and Barry McCrea work closely with our students, presenting the undergraduates with high-calibre learning and mentoring. In recent semesters, students can study Irish history from 1798 to the present from Kevin Whelan, and Modern Irish Literature from Declan Kiberd and Barry McCrea. The Dublin programme fosters an atmosphere in which Notre Dame students in any course of study can flourish and reach their fullest intellectual potential.

By working with their advisers at Notre Dame and in Dublin, students are able to create an Irish timetable which best complements their ND curriculum. Building upon their coursework, undergraduates collaborate with their academic mentors and locate faculty in their host institutions with whom they can conduct research. Additionally, many students acquire elite internship positions while in Dublin; whether working in the office of an Irish senator or conducting interviews for a potential senior thesis, these opportunities extend students' immersion in Irish life beyond the classroom, and affords them an undeniable advantage in future job applicant pools.

Friendships form on West of Ireland fieldtrips.

ND students are always competitive: skimming stones at Kylemore Abbey.

In 2009 these opportunities were incorporated into ND's Dublin curriculum in a more formal manner. Resulting from a new partnership with Notre Dame's Center for Social Concerns, the Dublin Centre added a Community-Based Learning (CBL) component to Kevin Whelan's 'Introduction to Ireland' course. Through this outreach, students are assigned to various community agencies throughout Dublin. By working with unaccompanied minors at Separated Children Educational Service, helping with after-school programming at the Aisling Project, or assisting Dublin's senior population through Friends of the Elderly, students are able to incorporate everyday experiences into their coursework. These students penetrate beneath the surface to gain a more in-depth understanding of Irish life. They stop being mere tourists, and they integrate their studies and their volunteering in a reflective and intentional manner.

Students' immersion into Ireland does not end with their coursework. Incorporating a full slate of cultural events, fieldtrips and activities, the Dublin programme exhorts students to learn 'through the soles of their feet' about the country. From the moment that the students get off the plane from America, they are encouraged to become actively involved in a host of events throughout the city and country. Almost immediately, the students are bound for the west of Ireland or Belfast on one of two weekend programme trips. Designed to expose the students to Ireland past and present, rural and urban, and accompanied by knowledgeable Irish scholars, these fieldtrips allow the students to study Ireland up-close and personal. They begin to see the country rather than just look at it.

Domers have climbed the pilgrim mountain of Croagh Patrick, hiked along Atlantic cliffs on the Aran Islands, and explored archaeology in the Burren. On trips West, they routinely engage with the community, through attending Irish language liturgies, sharing their musical talents during a session in the local pub, or learning hurling and Gaelic

Notre Dame students Spring 2011 display their musical talents in a 'Celtic Twilight' concert each semester.

Katie Carney, Linda Scheiber, Rachael Palumbo and Conor Hawes as the Dublin Double-Decker Bus. Fall 2011.

Audrey Vitter as 58 Merrion Square. Fall 2011.

The Macedonian Phalanx. O'Connell's metaphor is embodied in O'Connell House. Fall 2009.

football from the GAA club. A central aspect of all the trips is to have with us knowledgeable locally based guides. Peter Maguire and Noel Large in Belfast, Aidan Gough in Newry, Billy Colfer in Wexford, Mick Gibbons in Connemara, and Jack Burtchaell in Kilkenny have added enormously to the field trip experience.

The haunting murals and Peace Walls of Belfast and Derry powerfully move the students on every trip to Northern Ireland, where they learn the intricacies of the Troubles, and about the divided societies which endure to present day. Undergraduates have engaged with politicians from both nationalist and unionist backgrounds, questioning them about their pasts, their roles in the Troubles, and their vision for the future. Discovering that the people whom they meet may have been directly engaged in the violence that they study in their history classes brings the lesson vividly alive for our students. On their northern exposure, students also get to explore one of the stunning natural wonders of the world – the Giant's Causeway. At every step, students are encouraged to interrogate their predetermined notions of the world, to observe closely, to ask probing questions, and to soak in as much of the experience as they possibly can. The tiredness goes, but the memories remain.

Between and beyond the two trips, students are offered multiple opportunities for engaging with all facets of the life of Dublin – social, cultural, spiritual, musical, literary, sporting. After starting the semester with a practical walking tour – and a scavenger hunt – of Dublin, students are also led on literary tours of the city. Tours continue into Leinster House, home of the Irish Parliament. Senator Mark Daly guides our students through the parliamentary chambers, while fascinating them with stories, both Irish and American. Each semester includes trips to the magnificent theatres of Dublin – the Abbey, the Gate, the Gaiety – to experience classic and new works of Irish drama.

Not everything is serious or historical; experiencing a new city should also involve fun, and immersion in the rituals of the place. Each Christmas, our students attend the Irish tradition of the pantomime. They never quite know what to expect – what has Katy Perry to do with Robinson Crusoe? – but they inevitably have a smile on their face after experiencing this venerable Dublin custom. Students cheer on Dublin, Leinster, and Ireland at hurling and Gaelic football matches,

Martin Naughton, our generous Irish host, enjoys wearing a Native American headdress alongside ND student McKenzie Kennedy. Fall 2008.

rugby, and soccer games. They might not appreciate all the intricacies of these sports, but that does not stop them from becoming vehement fans, or enjoying the occasion and the banter with the Irish fans, who are always intrigued by the presence of a group of enthusiastic Americans. Ireland jerseys – conveniently green – become popular among Dublin alums, and can often be spotted at tailgates and transatlantic game watches.

In addition to these common features, autumn and spring semesters each present unique opportunities for the students. Away during football season and Thanksgiving, the Dublin programme has found ways to bring both to the students. Saturday nights in the fall find the O'Connell House classrooms transformed into the stadium student section, as the undergrads show up in 'The Shirt', living and dying with each reception and sack. In good years, the students get worn out from the number of push-ups they perform (carefully avoiding our Waterford-glass chandelier!). Thanks to programme benefactor Martin Naughton, what was once a depressing night away from family for American Thanksgiving has now been transformed into everyone's favourite night of the year. Dressed in their finest, the students are welcomed to Dublin's most elite hotel, the Merrion, for Mass and a superb dinner, always concluded with 'shaking down the thunder' as the students sing the *Notre Dame Victory March*.

Friends and family flood into Dublin in the spring, eager to get a taste of Ireland during its signature festival: Saint Patrick's Day. The day anchors a week of festivities, including carnivals, an enormous céilí, the hurling and Gaelic football finals in Croke Park, and the parade. This featured an appearance by the Notre Dame Marching Band in 2012, whose enthusiastic performance won them the 'Spirit of the Parade' Award. On the eve of St. Patrick's Day, O'Connell House is full of music, dancing, poetry, and traditional Irish food for the annual Celtic Twilight celebration. A night that allows our students to display their musical talents, it brings together the Notre Dame family before the city-wide celebrations.

Easter in Dublin finds the students departing for another reunion of the Notre Dame family, but this time in Rome. Domers have the privilege of spending the Easter holiday in the Eternal City, joining thousands of other Catholics at the Vatican for Easter Mass, praying on the Scala Sancti on Good Friday, and attending the Stations of the Cross with the Pope at the Colosseum. Hundreds of Notre Dame undergrads converge on Rome, praying beneath the Notre Dame flag all across the city.

Students grow and learn through their activities in Dublin but they also officially share, discuss, and teach with their classmates on topics in which they have a specialist interest. O'Connell House began 'Dublin Your Knowledge' in 2007, a weekly forum where students can speak about any topic of their choosing. This provides a learning opportunity that is student-led rather than professor-led. Students have presented on brain surgery, the chemistry of baking, the Korean War, flash animation, contemporary moral philosophy, astronomy, counter-culture, game theory in insurgent conflicts, and so much more. The insightful discussions during 'Dublin Your Knowledge' enrich the quality of their education, pushing students to always think outside the box and to have intellectual conversations.

Through 'Dublin Your Knowledge' and myriad other programme events, the Dublin Programme encourages our students to engage in conversation with the people that they encounter, to appreciate the differences between America and Ireland that make each nation unique, and to be open always to the latent and ubiquitous opportunities to learn something new.

Monica Bushman and her parents on St. Patrick's Day 2005 in Dublin.

St. Patrick (aka Nick Mancinelli) puts in an appearance at O'Connell House. Spring 2010

From the Heart: Emilee Booth Chapman, Dublin Fall 2007

In 2007 I went to Dublin intending to study Irish literature. During my first two years at Notre Dame, I had become somewhat unsatisfied with my work as an English major, but I had fallen in love with Irish literature and with the Irish language. I was certain that going to the source of it would give me a renewed sense of academic purpose, and so I signed up for three English literature courses at UCD, including a seminar on the Irish playwright Brian Friel. While I found these classes interesting, it was a casual elective, a political theory course simply titled International Justice, that most captured my attention. In this class I discovered that what most attracted me to Irish literature were the kinds of political questions it so often raised: Do people have a right to a culture or a way of life? Does a person owe more to her fellow citizens than to non-citizens? What gives a person or group the right to exercise political authority over a piece of land? Political theory enabled me to engage with these debates directly, and I felt I could contribute to the field in a way I never thought I could with the study of literature.

I returned to Dublin for an internship with the Irish government agency Combat Poverty in the summer of 2008, still recognising the general questions about the ethics of public life animating Irish politics. By the time I started my senior year at Notre Dame, I was confident enough in my new field to devote that fall to applying to political theory graduate programs, and I am now halfway through a political theory Ph. D. at Princeton, still convinced that I have made the best decision.

My time in Dublin did not just introduce me to my field, though. It helped me discover the independence and confidence I needed to radically change the direction of my academic career more than halfway through my time at Notre Dame, to approach faculty I had never met for advice and favours, and to convince my advisors that I was committed to my new field and prepared to pursue a graduate degree in political theory.

Even still, my time in Dublin gave me something far more important than a new career path. I made many new friends among my fellow students, and I still count a few of them as my closest friends. Last summer, I even married one of them. We spent our honeymoon in Ireland, of course.

While they build upon all of these events and trips, every student who passes through Dublin has a unique story to tell about their experience. For some, it's about drinking a pint of the black stuff in each of the island's thirty-two counties. For others, it is about discovering their lifelong passion, whether it be through a class or a trip, or through the people that they encounter. Cupid is particularly busy in Ireland. At least forty of our students have met their future spouse during their Dublin semester, a statistic that sparks nervous laughter and furtive glances about the room from every new student with whom it is shared.

Throughout the semester, students continue to build a community. While they discover friendships with their Irish and international classmates, they inevitably bond most with their fellow Domers. Spring 2007 student Ginna Dybicz realised just how close she had become with other Dubliners when she returned to campus: 'I was eating dinner with my friends from the dorm the other night, and one of the girls asked me, 'Did you know any of the Dublin kids before you went abroad? Because you spend an awful lot of time with them'. I told her that I only knew two of my classmates before Dublin, and she was impressed. That's quite a testament to my abroad experience'.

As the end of the semester approaches, students are shocked to discover that the thing they have learned the most about during their semester is themselves. It is usually just prior to departure that the students recognise their personal transformations. They have lived on their own, travelled internationally, and navigated successfully an alien education system. They realise that their original impressions, ideas and expectations of their study abroad experience has been infused, enriched and ultimately preserved by real moments in time that they never could have anticipated and that they never will forget: though nervous when they arrive, many request us to suggest ways that they can stay when the time comes to leave.

The Dublin experience ultimately gives our students the confidence to take on new challenges and to pursue ambitiously their goals in research, education, employment, and most importantly of all life. They go back with a lust for travel, for experiencing new things and for stretching themselves. They come with stereotypes: they go home with knowledge.

Brian Corrigan (ND Dublin '08) shows the young ones how it's done: Saint Louis School, Rathmines.

Declan Kiberd cuts a 90th birthday cake for *Ulyssses,* 2012.

Carlene Koken interacts with Tom Hartley, Lord Mayor of Belfast, 2009.

Christmas in Dublin 03: Back row: Lauren Flynn, Suzy Cotter, Michael Johnston, Carol Weber, Molly Welch. Middle row: Andrew Remick, Kristin Boyd, Ashlee (O'Donnell) Barrett, Erin (Sheehan) Phinney, Nell Ryan. Front row: Erin Ennes, Ashley Merusi.

Painting a mural at St. Louis School, Rathmines. The white suits protect the students' clothes.

Spring 2010 students Nicki Allen and Jacquie Thomas share a smile at Friends of the Elderly.

From the Heart: Andrew Hoyt, Dublin 2003–04

The problem was the price. I remember standing in the Hodges Figgis Bookstore on Dawson Street and holding the thing in my hand. It was enormous. A behemoth. It cost something like twenty-five Euros (in paperback), which was beyond my comprehension. I was a poor college student, spending the year abroad in the expensive city of Dublin, Ireland, and there was no way I could afford it.

I took the book off the shelf and flipped to the opening page. *God* it was heavy. After a few minutes, I was sitting down in the middle of the aisle, turning pages. About fifteen minutes after that, I got back up, went a few aisles over, and retrieved a dictionary. Then I sat back down and kept reading. I left the bookstore that day with a firm resolution: I would read the whole thing without paying for it.

After the first week, I started to get paranoid that the clerks in Hodges Figgis were onto me. Luckily, there was another bookstore, Waterstone's, directly across the street. So I devised and enacted a detailed system of rotations between the two bookstores during my walks to and from classes. The rule was simple: I never went into the same store during the same shift on any two consecutive days.

Obviously, I ended up in love. The kind of love that makes you sit on the carpet of Hodges Figgis, crammed between the stacks with a neck cramp and a numb ass. I was faithful; I showed up everyday with my dictionary ready and coffee in hand. I fell in love like most of you probably did, and met that book twice a day for lovers' trysts amidst the cramped corridors of bookshelves. Both stores had exactly one copy of *Infinite Jest*, so you could observe the progress of my love affair through the creases on the spine of the book.

I snuck into the bookstores, hoping not to be recognised, and reminding myself not to walk straight through the door and to the *Jest*. Try to be calm, look at a few bestsellers – act *cool*. As soon as you're sure that you aren't drawing any attention, slowly drift your way over to the familiar aisle. Getting to the book was an art form and a game.

I wore a fake moustache on at least two occasions. I made it more than 600 pages into *Infinite Jest* without removing it from the bookstore. And that's not counting footnotes, obviously. Then, unexpectedly, I went into Hodges Figgis one afternoon and it was gone. No way. No *way*. I was devastated. I remember moving the books around with my hand, as if I expected to see it had just slipped behind them somehow or something. It hadn't. It was gone.

I had just been in Waterstone's earlier and obviously couldn't go back, since it wasn't late enough in the afternoon for the shift to have changed. Not only that, with only one copy of the book remaining, there would be no way to continue with my reading times. This was a disaster.

I walked back to my flat dejected, wondering what Dubliner was thumbing through it in his own personal home that evening, and when I got back it was sitting on my bed.

My friend Patrick bought it for me in a move that still impresses me to do this day. He had given me a fantastic gift, pages I was already in love with, and raised also a tremendous middle finger, ruining my opportunity to say to future friends that I completed *Infinite Jest* entirely in the confines of the bookstore. It was genius, of course. It is true that the book and the writer changed my life, but I won't try to sum up just how. I will say that I own five copies of that book now, and that he was my hero.

IRISH SEMINAR THEMES 1999–2012

- 1999 Memory and History: Ireland 1500–2000
- 2000 Modern Ireland 1880–1930
- 2001 Contemporary Ireland
- 2002 Ireland and Globalisation
- 2003 The Irish Body
- 2004 Boston or Berlin?
- 2005 Genealogies of Culture
- 2006 Capitals of Culture: Paris and Dublin
- 2007 Irish Classics
- 2008 Republics and Empires
- 2009 Apocalypse and Utopia
- 2010 The Irish Revival
- 2011 Irish Modernisms
- 2012 Contemporary Irish Theatre

Glenmalure Field Trip,
Irish Seminar 2010.

THE MADDEN-ROONEY PUBLIC LECTURES

GENEALOGIES OF CULTURE

TUESDAY 28 JUNE	**HOMI BHABHA**	"A SCRAMBLED EGG AND A DISH OF RICE": INTERNATIONAL NATIONALISM & THE GENEALOGY OF MINORITISATION
TUESDAY 5 JULY	**MAUD ELLMANN**	*ULYSSES*: TURNING INTO AN ANIMAL
TUESDAY 12 JULY	**SIOBHAN KILFEATHER**	GENEALOGIES OF IRISH FEMINISM

IRISH SEMINAR 2005 • KEOUGH NOTRE DAME CENTRE

ALL LECTURES ARE AT 8 pm IN ROOM G 32, EARLSFORT TERRACE.
LECTURES ARE FREE AND OPEN TO THE PUBLIC.
TO BOOK SEATS, PLEASE CONTACT CAROLINE MOLONEY: 611 0554.
E MAIL irishsem@nd.edu • WEBSITE www.nd.edu/~irishsem

From the Heart: Deb Rotman, Director of the Center for Undergraduate Scholarly Engagement, Notre Dame

When I joined the faculty at Notre Dame in 2006, I wondered, 'How did a university with a French name become the Fighting Irish?' Thus began a dynamic transnational investigation of the Irish diaspora in America. My students and I seek to understand *ethnogenesis* (the process of forming new cultural identities) and the transition from being Irish to becoming Irish-American.

Using archival records, archaeological data, and oral histories in both Ireland and the United States, we initially explored the early history of Notre Dame and its connections to the local Irish immigrant community. Fr. Sorin was seeking Catholic workers to build the University in the 1840s and 1850s, at a time when Famine immigrants were flooding into the US. Fr. Sorin purchased a 120-acre tract of land ('Sorinsville') south of campus in 1855. Smaller parcels of this tract were sold for a $25 down payment, with the balance repaid through barter, trade or long-term credit agreement.

These Irish Catholic workers served the University as bricklayers, carpenters and labourers. My archaeological excavation in their neighbourhood illustrated that these Irish families selectively embraced some local cultural norms while rejecting others. The material evidence also elucidated each family's unique process of becoming Irish-American in South Bend, where supportive Catholic infrastructure facilitated their assimilation.

In 2009, we began exploring the extraordinary Irish enclave of Beaver Island in northern Lake Michigan, the population of which was almost exclusively derived from Árainn Mhór, an island off the coast of County Donegal. Indeed, Beaver Island became one of the very few American immigrant communities to remain an Irish-speaking area from 1856 until 1903. Discovering that unique linguistic inheritance has encouraged me to learn Irish myself. These fishermen-farmers from the Irish Atlantic coast were also able to continue being fishermen-farmers in the Great Lakes area: by contrast, their counterparts on the eastern seaboard had to abandon traditional lifeways when they became factory workers and day labourers in the cities.

Our continuing investigations on Beaver Island illustrate how these Irish families navigated the multifaceted and ever-changing social landscapes in which they lived, continuing some traditions from their homeland while incorporating new cultural practices. Undergraduate students are active research collaborators on this project in every way, conducting archival research and collecting oral histories on both sides of the Atlantic. In summer 2011, I travelled with a dozen students to the *Gaeltacht* (Irish-speaking) regions of western Ireland to study the rituals, beliefs and norms that immigrants would have brought with them to the US.

We also excavated the yards around nineteenth-century Irish immigrant home on Beaver Island and analysed the artifacts and other archaeological evidence that we recovered. Through their scholarly engagement in this project, students acquire robust research skills, learning outside the classroom in ways that distinguish them from their peers and prepare them for future success. It is a privilege for me to enable these talented Notre Dame students to experience Irish and Irish-American culture up close and personal.

DUBLIN INTERNSHIPS

Don Keough has generously supported the Keough Interns in Ireland. Back in 1996, the very first of them, now Fr. Sean McGraw, CSC, worked with Alan Dukes (former leader of Fine Gael, the Irish political party). Sean is still immersed in contemporary Irish politics, having completing a doctoral thesis on the subject at Harvard, before he joined the ND faculty in 2009.

The generosity of Ireland Council members makes it possible to award internships in Dublin to promising rising seniors each summer. Some internships are reserved for students minoring in Irish Studies.

These Irish internships place undergrads in positions in Dublin relating to politics, commerce, culture and social service, allowing talented ND students to participate in various work environments. Internships last for seven weeks each summer during which time the students are under the guidance of Eimear Clowry, Internship Co-Ordinator at the Keough Naughton Dublin Centre. Successful candidates receive a round-trip airfare from the United States to Ireland, accommodation, and a living stipend for the duration of their stay. Before the end of July, the Interns submit a written evaluation of their experience to the Director of the Keough Naughton Institute.

Since 2001, Keough Interns have served in a variety of prominent Irish institutions – government departments, galleries, libraries, archives, museums, not-for-profits, cultural bodies, publishing houses, Irish language organisations, theatres, political parties, architectural practices and archaeological excavations

In 2012, two new sets of internships became available. The DISC (Dublin Internship in Social Concerns) internships are co-funded by the Centre for Social Concerns, the Nanovic Institute and the Keough Naughton Centre Dublin. The I-NURF (Irish Naughton Undergraduate Research Fellowships) allow ND Science, Technology, Engineering and Mathematics students to intern in laboratories at TCD and University College Cork. These multiple internships offer ND students a wide array of exciting possibilities across a range of activities.

ND Keough interns in Dublin Summer 2012: Caitlin Myron, Athena Hughes, Laura Kraegel, Abby McCrary, Katie Rose and Josh Whitaker.

2011 Keough Interns Kelly Fallon, Kari Johnson, Hilary Kelly, Annie Cassel, Anne Whitty and Tyler Harmsen after taking a dip at the Forty Foot to start Bloomsday.

Full Immersion: Taking the plunge at Joyce's Tower, Bloomsday, June 2011.

A group of ND interns in Summer 2012: Front Row: Monica McNerney, Alexa Solazzo (ND Dublin '11), Abby McCrary, Katie Rose (DSP '11), Katie Carney (ND Dublin '11); Back Row: Laura Kraegel, Michael Collins (ND Dublin '12), Josh Whitaker (DSP '11), Pat McCoy (ND Dublin '08-'09), Athena Hughes (ND Dublin '12), Caitlin Myron (ND Dublin '11-'12).

NOTRE DAME INTERNS IN DUBLIN

2001
Suzanne Kellmann: Irish Museum of Modern Art
Julia Koslow: Paul Keogh Architects
John Scully: Department of Foreign Affairs
Josh Warner: Jobstown Community Initiative

2002
Bridget O'Brien: National Gallery of Ireland
Bill Boyd: Department of Foreign Affairs
Seth Whetzel: Archaeological Excavation, Boyne Valley
Maureen Jones: Pavilion Theatre, Dún Laoghaire
Kathryn Hylden: Missionaries of Charity
Chris Sanders: SEI Investments

2003
Shannon Byrne: Department of Foreign Affairs
Eileen Carroll: Combat Poverty Agency
Cara Sheil: National Gallery of Ireland
Aidan Brett: Archaeological Excavation, Newgrange
Kate Murphy: Department of Foreign Affairs
Jim Krenn: SEI Investments

2004
Maeve Carey: Department of Foreign Affairs
Elizabeth Doyle: Chester Beatty Library
Nicole Rogers: Electronics & Engineering Department, TCD
Russell Morton: Applied Physics Department, TCD
Mark Guest: Combat Poverty Agency

2005
Claire Kelly: Field Day Publishing
Joey Minta: Department of Justice & Equality
Mike McGinley: Department of Foreign Affairs
Megan Conroy: Irish Film Institute
Laura Murphy Heslin: Combat Poverty Agency

2006
Emily Krisciunas: National Gallery of Ireland
Áine Richards: Department of Justice
Christina O'Donnell: Department of Foreign Affairs
Caroline Murphy: Combat Poverty Agency
Teresa De Vries: Press Section, European Commission

2007
Martha Ehlenbach: Foras na Gaeilge
Michael O'Connor: Field Day Publishing
Andrea Laidman: Department of Justice & Equality
Jessica Morton: Poetry Ireland
Lauren McDonough: Comhaltas Ceolteóiri na hÉireann
Patrick Lasseter: Pavee Point Travellers Centre

2008
Margaret Emilee Booth: Combat Poverty
Maria Paula Elizondo: EU Commission
Mallory Meecham: McCullough Mulvin Architects
Gary Nijak: Purification Engineering, Dublin City University
Kelly Clancy: Goal (Third World agency)
Stephen Iwanski: Pavilion Theatre, Dun Laoghaire

2009
Sarah Carruthers: Tús Nua, DePaul Ireland
Patrick McCoy: Royal Irish Academy
Beth Neiman: Equality Tribunal, Department of Justice
Anthony Parrish: Abbey Theatre
Gwendolyn Rugg: National Gallery of Ireland
Kaitlin Sullivan: Department of Foreign Affairs

2010
Claire Brosnihan: Department of Justice & Equality
Paul Dechant: Irish Film Institute
Erica Pepitone: Poetry Ireland
Rochelle Rieger: Department of Foreign Affairs
Amanda Springstead: Festina Lente (Equitation centre)
Joanna Thurnes: National Gallery of Ireland

2011
Annie Cassel: Abbey Theatre
Kelly Fallon: National Gallery of Ireland
Tyler Harmsen: Focus Ireland (Homeless charity)
Kari Johnson: Olympic Council of Ireland
Hilary Kelly: Department of Foreign Affairs
Anne Whitty: Environmental Protection Agency

2012

Keough Interns

Abigail McCrary: Bord Bia
Laura Kraegel: Poetry Ireland
Caitlin Myron: Foras na Gaeilge
Joshua Whitaker: Four Courts Press
Athena Hughes: Department of Foreign Affairs
Katie Rose: Department of Foreign Affairs

Dublin Internships in Social Concerns

Katie Carney: Friends of the Elderly
Alexa Solazzo: Le Chéile Catholic Education Trust

Irish Naughton Undergraduate Research Fellowships

Marissa Gaskill: UCC
Hayley Hilton: UCC
Sarah Krug : UCC
Michael Collins: TCD
Monica McNerney: TCD

Summer Programme 2012 with Kevin Whelan and Deb Rotman in Merrion Square.

DUBLIN SUMMER PROGRAMME

Established in summer 2011, the Dublin Summer Programme provides ND undergraduates with an intense summer immersion experience at O'Connell House. Twenty-six students live in Dublin for six weeks each summer, studying Irish history and culture with a rotating pair of ND professors. The inaugural session was led by Bob Schmuhl of American Studies and Kevin Whelan of the Keough Naughton Dublin Centre. Deb Rotman of Anthropology and the Center for Undergraduate Scholarly Engagement joined the faculty for the second summer.

Believing that students will learn just as much from their experiences as in the classroom, the programme takes advantage of the unique opportunities provided by its Dublin base. Students partake in a full cultural programme, including trips throughout Ireland, tours of museums, theatres and galleries, guest lectures, sporting events, and film screenings. Students also attend musical and theatrical performances in Dublin's best-known venues.

Declan Kiberd joins the group for a 2011 fieldtrip to Hook Head, County Wexford.

While learning about James Joyce and the significance of *Ulysses*, students live out the first pages of the novel by swimming at Sandycove and following in the footsteps of Leopold Bloom on Bloomsday. Following their lectures on Northern Ireland, they venture into Belfast, beginning to understand the human element of the Troubles. Putting Irish history in a broader historical context, they journey to the early medieval monastic city at Glendalough and the 5,000 year old passage tombs at Newgrange and Knowth. In 2012, a week-long trip to the Burren was introduced, immersing students in the grey limestone hills, the archaeological landscape of the west of Ireland, and becoming part of village life in Ballyvaughan.

Dublin Summer Programme 2011 celebrates American Independence Day at Drumleck, with Fergal and Rachael Naughton.

Tom and Eleanor Kinsella join Elizabeth Wassell and John Montague at the launch of Montague's *New Collected Poems* in O'Connell House, June 2012.

To have such a programme in Irish Studies, which is so important to Notre Dame, makes it one of the jewels in the crown of Notre Dame.

FR. JOHN JENKINS, CSC, PRESIDENT OF NOTRE DAME

Over one thousand students have passed through Dublin, learning about the country, continuing their studies, and becoming ambassadors for Ireland wherever they have gone.

TOM BURISH, PROVOST OF NOTRE DAME

Participants in the Dublin Summer Programme 2012 listen attentively in historic Green Street Courthouse: L to R: Connor Sullivan, Alexandra Janiw, Sarah Doyle, Taylor Boyd, Colleen McCartney, Catherine Ake, Olivia Kacsits, Kelsey Eckenrode.

The thought of Irish Studies kept coming into my mind. Here was this place, Notre Dame, which was truly Irish. I wanted to work with the University, to start an Irish Studies Programme. It's amazing, isn't it, when you start something, when you push that forward, how far you can go.

DON KEOUGH

Don Keough's dream was of creating a world-rated programme, not just any old programme. I was attracted to that push for excellence. The programme is now attracting the best of the best, and it's just been so exciting to watch it flourish.

MARTIN NAUGHTON

Each year a group gathers to honour Bloomsday under the auspices of the Keough Naughton Centre. Michael Fitzgerald, Felim Egan, Edna O'Brien, Basil Blackshaw, Seamus Deane, Kevin Whelan, and Stephen Rea at Newman House 2003.

At the Merrion Hotel 2011: a group including Stephen Rea, Philip King, Neil Jordan, Fiach Mac Conghail, John Boorman, Gabriel Byrne, Brendan Gleeson and Maighreád Ní Dhomhnaill.

TUNDISH AWARD WINNERS

2000	**Edna O'Brien:** novelist
2001	**Thomas Kinsella:** poet
2002	**Tom Kilroy:** dramatist
2003	**Basil Blackshaw:** artist
2004	**John McGahern:** novelist
2004	**Haruki Murakami:** novelist
2005	**Seamus Deane:** scholar
2006	**Sineád Cusack:** actor
2007	**Liam O'Flynn:** uilleann piper
2008	**Philip King:** musician
2009	**Sam Shepard:** dramatist
2010	**Seán Scully:** artist
2011	**John Boorman:** film-maker
2012	**Maighreád Ní Dhomhnaill:** singer

The Award is given for a distinguished lifetime contribution to culture

From the Heart: Elizabeth Moore, Dublin Spring 2012

My eyes widened in excitement as I looked down on a barely legible, century-old ledger. Scanning the titles of script submissions to the Abbey, Ireland's national theatre, I recognised plays and authors, now performed and studied with banal frequency, then unseen by the public, unknown artists looking for their start. I saw William Butler Yeats' signature on Board meeting minutes. My personal connection to the history of the Abbey and of Ireland was so tangible in those moments.

During my semester in Dublin, I interned at the Abbey in the literary department. All undergraduate interns appreciate their close relationship with the photocopy machine, and the subtle art of stuffing envelopes. I relished the opportunity to help in any way that I could. As I worked, I felt part of the continuing process of the theatre, from initial script submission, to contact with new and established writers, and (occasionally, miraculously) watching the performance on stage.

The Abbey receives hundreds of unsolicited scripts each year and the literary department must read and respond constructively to every writer. I immersed myself in this process, fielding queries via email, as well as filing and organising the scripts and correspondence. With each script came the tantalising possibility of encountering something unique, lasting, magical that might have the capacity to enter the rich canon of Irish drama. As I went through each submission, tracking the writer and the Abbey's response, I felt myself connected right back to Yeats and his original ledger.

These imaginative connections to the past made my time at the Abbey inimitable. My experience in Ireland expanded personal memories of the past (my father grew up in Waterford) but also my ND experience, as I bonded with other students far away from the comforting, familiar, insular campus. We stretched ourselves and supported each other as we journeyed through our new world. As an English major, I challenged myself to see beyond the words of a drama, and immerse myself in the theatre environment where the script is merely the beginning. My Dublin and Abbey experience connected me to what I most cherished about Irish culture. By embracing the opportunity, I gained new insights into ND, Ireland, literature but above all into myself and my Irish family.

FIELD DAY

Brian Friel and Stephen Rea established Field Day as a theatre company in 1980. Beginning with Friel's *Translations* (1980), the company produced and toured over a dozen plays, including world premières of Friel's *The Communication Cord* (1982) and *Making History* (1988), Derek Mahon's *High Time* (1984), Tom Paulin's *The Riot Act* (1984), Tom Kilroy's *Double Cross* (1986), Stewart Parker's *Pentecost* (1987), and Seamus Heaney's *The Cure at Troy* (1990). In 1980, Friel's superb play *Translations* was premiered in Derry with the hope of establishing a major theatre company for Northern Ireland. After the production, Seamus Heaney commented: 'this was what theatre was supposed to do'.

Although Field Day never issued a formal mission statement, their intention was to create a space that transcended the crippling oppositions of Irish politics. It quickly grew into a much larger cultural and political project. Four Northern Irish writers joined the project – Seamus Deane, David Hammond, Seamus Heaney and Tom Paulin (Tom Kilroy, the only member from the Republic, joined in 1988). Field Day aimed to contribute to the solution of the present crisis by analysing embedded stereotypes which had become both a symptom and a cause of the current situation. It began publishing pamphlets 'in which the nature of the Irish problem could be explored and, as a result, more successfully confronted than it had been hitherto'. Field Day Pamphlets (1983-1988) offered fifteen essays on culture and politics by, amongst others, Seamus Deane, Fredric Jameson, Tom Paulin, Declan Kiberd and Edward Said. It also published *The Field Day Anthology of Irish Writing*, in five volumes (1991, 2002), edited by Seamus Deane. According to Deane, the anthology was an 'act of definition', seeking to be inclusive and representative of the plurality of Irish identities. Field Day also published *Critical Conditions* (1996-2005), fifteen essay collections on issues in Irish cultural studies, which included books by David Lloyd, Joop Leerssen, Clare O'Halloran, Elizabeth Cullingford, Clare Carroll and Kevin Whelan.

The Bloomsday Celebraion outside Shakespeare and Company bookshop in Paris 2004. Back Row: Pierre Joannon, Kevin Whelan, Mike Fitzgerald, Felim Egan. Front Row: Seamus Deane, Edna O'Brien, Stephen Rea, Emer Nolan, Maggie Fitzgerald.

In 2005, Field Day Publications was launched in association with the Keough-Naughton Institute for Irish Studies. With Seamus Deane as General Editor, *Field Day Review* (2005-) is an annual journal primarily concerned with Irish literary and political culture. It has attracted essays by major global scholars. Field Day Publications has also published twenty-one titles since it started its collaboration with the Keough-Naughton Institute for Irish Studies.

From the Heart: Seamus Deane, Emeritus Keough Professor

Irish Studies is a relatively new field in the institutional sense. It can be a Centre, an Institute, an Area Studies, or merely a Concentration, but nowhere is there a free-standing Department of Irish Studies. It's always in an arm-link with something else; the title 'Studies', honourable in itself, nevertheless always implies a relationship that may be steady at the core but nervous around the edges or even nervous all the way through. That's true of many fields; indeed it perhaps should be true of all. Every arrow that hits a solid target quivers for some time with the force of its own velocity as well as of the target's solidity. And everything that was ever solid melts and reforms itself in the pressured air of research and speculation. The arrow keeps on travelling.

I was a member of the Field Day Company, founded in 1980, that bent the bow and the string for the release of that arrow. It took a deal of strength and skill to get it on target, but we had that in plenty with Stephen Rea, Seamus Heaney and Brian Friel among the founding members and participants. In the Fall of 1993, I initiated the Irish Studies Programme at the University of Notre Dame. First it was an idea, then it was an option for those studying English or History, then it was an area of study, a concentration, a Centre, finally an Institute. The arrow was not then flying through the heavily polluted air of Northern Ireland and it still does meet now some resistance, although I think we can at last say that much of that resistance is coming from the reluctance of the target to reform itself under the impact of the work that has been done in the last thirty years or so.

This is natural. But in each phase of its development, what we now call Irish Studies had to cope with new conditions, the most pressing of which were themselves the product of its own arrival. With Field Day we had theatre and publications; with Notre Dame, we had teaching, library development, research and in the last decade we achieved a convergence of the two with publications dedicated to the enlargement, interrogation and enrichment of the whole enterprise. The annual *Field Day Review*, now in its eighth number, and the various monographs and editions – including editions in Irish of some of the most important poets of the tradition – bring to the Irish Institute at the University of Notre Dame the prestige and the pioneering spirit of the Field Day Company of the 1980-1992 period. In return, the University of Notre Dame has provided an academic prestige for the whole enterprise. It is in the publications that the quality and scale of what Irish Studies has achieved and can achieve is becoming ever more visible. Our ambit has widened beyond literature and history to music and painting, folklore, economics, and the various combinations of these that operate in the contemporary world's contemplation of itself and its past.

The list of eminent intellectuals, both in Irish Studies and beyond, who have published in the *Field Day Review*, is a tribute to the amplitude of our achievement; among them Toril Moi, Pascale Casanova, Fredric Jameson, David Lloyd, Joe Cleary, Siobhán Kilfeather, Terry Eagleton, Benedict Anderson, Katie Trumpener, Maud Ellmann and Giovanni Arrighi. The aim is to make what we are doing ever more visible and ever more lustrous. Field Day and Notre Dame have been a powerful and winning combination.

'Publish or Perish' was once the command and threat that governed the world of the young academic. Although changes in technology have made the idea of publication different from what it once was, the imperative still has force. The articles in the *Field Day Review* can be read online, for instance, and we have, of course, our own website. But the opportunities as well as the challenges of that dizzying new world have to be met and the distinctions between information and knowledge have to be made. Otherwise, unless we learn to live in the virtual world, our achievements will not be made actual. In that sense, we publish or we perish.

Searching for shamrock on Slane Hill,
where St. Patrick lit the Paschal fire.

NOTRE DAME'S SPIRITUAL AND PASTORAL ROLE IN IRELAND

8

CHAPTER

NOTRE DAME'S SPIRITUAL AND PASTORAL ROLE IN IRELAND

The Keough Notre Dame Dublin Centre, as it then was, began life in 1998 on the top floor of Newman House on Stephen's Green, the home of Newman's Catholic University. It was an ideal homecoming for Notre Dame to Ireland, as Newman's philosophy of the harmonious blend of faith and intellect also underpins the mission of the University of Notre Dame. And to understand that philosophy, one needs to understand the intellectual trajectory and faith journey of this great leader, who was beatified on 19 September 2010 by Pope Benedict XVI.

John Henry Cardinal Newman (1801–1890), the son of a London banker, was a shy, sensitive man. He studied and worked at Oxford from 1816 to 1845, where he was ordained as an Anglican clergyman. Newman started the Oxford Movement there to revitalise English Anglicanism. Following his sensational conversion to Catholicism in 1845, he was ordained as a Catholic priest in Rome in 1847. The Catholic University was established in Dublin in 1852 and Newman was its Rector from 1854 to 1858. Newman was a consummate prose stylist. Even James Joyce was impressed despite himself: 'nobody has ever written English prose that can be compared with that of a tiresome footling little Anglican parson who afterwards became a prince of the only true church'.

John Cardinal Newman.

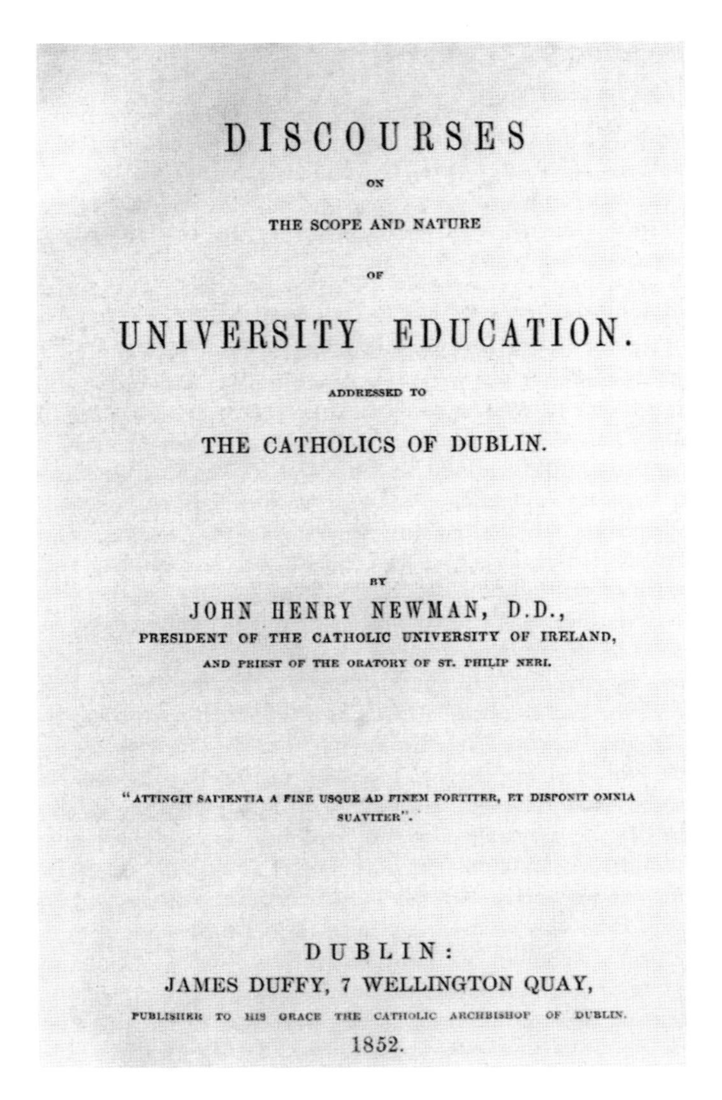

DISCOURSES

ON

THE SCOPE AND NATURE

OF

UNIVERSITY EDUCATION.

ADDRESSED TO

THE CATHOLICS OF DUBLIN.

BY

JOHN HENRY NEWMAN, D.D.,

PRESIDENT OF THE CATHOLIC UNIVERSITY OF IRELAND,

AND PRIEST OF THE ORATORY OF ST. PHILIP NERI.

"ATTINGIT SAPIENTIA A FINE USQUE AD FINEM FORTITER, ET DISPONIT OMNIA SUAVITER".

DUBLIN:

JAMES DUFFY, 7 WELLINGTON QUAY,

PUBLISHER TO HIS GRACE THE CATHOLIC ARCHBISHOP OF DUBLIN.

1852.

Cardinal Newman's *The Idea of a University* was was first delivered as a series of lectures in Dublin outlining his philosophy for the Catholic University.

SEDES SAPIENTIA

The front door of Newman House bears a (tin) lion over the architrave. The doorstep has been worn unevenly by the feet of those passing through – like James Joyce who was a student here.

Newman published the elegantly written *Apologia pro Vita Sua* in 1864 – an account of his life as an Anglican until 1845 and a lucid defence of his intellectual integrity. He had earlier written the well-known hymn 'Lead Kindly Light' in 1833. *The Dream of Gerontius* (1865), his profound and poetic meditation on old age, was brilliantly set to music by Elgar in 1900. Newman was elevated to Cardinal in 1879.

Newman belonged to the reaction to the French Revolution, making an explicit effort to reconnect with the older roots of European thought and its Christian heritage in religion, art and architecture. He opposed the corrosive effects of the rationalism of the Enlightenment: 'My battle was with liberalism, national apostasy and secularism'. Newman aphorised that 'Wonder is not religion or we should be worshipping railroads'. He sought to reconnect modern England with the Greek virtues rather than the Roman ones – the practical, getting and spending imperial values, which had corrupted the splendour of the early Republic, and which lay like the sword of Damocles over England as a warning to the materialist rapacity and acquisitiveness of the British Empire.

In 1852 in Dublin, he delivered the series of lectures that eventually became known as *The Idea of a University*. This was first published in Dublin by the Catholic publishing house James Duffy as *Discourses on the scope and nature of university education addressed to the Catholics of Dublin* (Dublin, 1852). The title was changed in the 1873 edition to *The Idea of a University defined and illustrated*. For Newman, the university obviously had to be a place for the teaching of knowledge but it needed

James Joyce in 1919. Joyce's undergraduate career was in Newman House, which features in Chapter 5 of *Portrait of the Artist as a Young Man*.

also to impart wisdom, seeking to educate the whole person. At the heart of the Chapel that he designed beside Newman House, Newman installed the Blessed Virgin/Notre Dame in her capacity as *sedes sapientia* (seat of wisdom) – not as *sedes scientiae* (seat of knowledge).

Newman was the most articulate advocate for the blend of faith and intellect that is the foundational Notre Dame tradition. He advocated that a university should not just be an academy dedicated solely to research nor a seminary dedicated solely to technical training. A university should meld theology and philosophy, for it existed to teach not just knowledge but also wisdom – the application of knowledge in the living of a good life. The university should never just dwindle into a purveyor of merely professional training for mercenary purposes:

> The man who has learned to think and to reason and to compare and to discriminate and to analyse, who has refined his taste and formed his judgement and sharpened his

> mental vision will be ... placed in that state of intellect in which he can take up any one of the sciences or the callings I have referred to or any other, with an ease, a grace, a versatility and a success, to which another is a stranger.

Arthur Clery (1879–1932), Joyce's contemporary, commented on how Newman made university education accessible to Irish Catholics:

> Remember who Newman was. If ever man could claim the title, he was the flower of English University culture, a culture highly refined but fiercely exclusive. By establishing facilities for university education for the man who was working for his daily bread, whom poverty or family need had sent forth to earn an early living, Newman broke with all the traditions of his time. He cast aside the Reformation and the Renaissance, and went back to the broader and nobler ideas of the Middle Ages, when daily toil and the highest learning were not looked upon as incompatible, when, in fact, the greatest minds of the monastic world regarded the one as the complement of the other. It was the Renaissance and Reformation civilisation which first made learning the special preserve of wealth, which divorced it from labour. And in most modern countries we find below a certain point an immense populace without clothes, without food, without faith; the phenomenon is closely connected with that policy which has made higher learning the preserve of the moneyed classes. Newman definitely broke with this policy. Within the restricted limits in which it was possible for him, he threw open the doors of learning, and many men, living and dead, with honoured names received their education at his classes.

As rector of the Catholic University on Stephen's Green, he commissioned what is now called Newman Chapel as a signature building to symbolise 'the great principle of the university, the indissoluble union of philosophy with religion'. Newman himself worked closely on its design with John Hungerford Pollen, his Professor of Fine Arts. When it opened in 1856, Newman was pleased: 'The church is the most beautiful one in the three Kingdoms'. It is one of the few Greek-inspired Catholic churches in an Ireland besotted with Roman models. Newman's choice of the Greek style was a self-conscious effort to elevate spiritual and intellectual over material and bureaucratic modes of thought. Newman Chapel has recently been restored.

SAINT PATRICK'S CHAPEL O'CONNELL HOUSE

Newman Chapel provided a historic and inspiring resource to Notre Dame students studying in Dublin, a place for reflection and prayer in the heart of a bustling city. To students coming from Notre Dame's campus – studded with chapels, the Grotto, and the Basilica of the Sacred Heart – Newman Chapel provided a familiar and relaxed escape. So when the University acquired O'Connell House and prepared to move away from Newman Chapel, it was natural to add a chapel to their new home – and to call it after the patron saint of Ireland. Saint Patrick's Chapel lies at the heart of O'Connell House, where the celebration of Mass is the sacrament of the communion and community that is the lifeblood of Notre Dame in Dublin. Always open for prayer, the chapel is a reminder of the warm and welcome spaces for prayer back on campus, and the gospel roots that ground the mission of the University. The intimate chapels in every residence hall were the inspiration for creating a similar space in O'Connell House.

Outside the door of the chapel, the Holy Water font is modelled on the tenth-century High Cross of Moone in County Kildare. Sculpted by Colm Brennan, it portrays in a stylised but striking manner the story of the loaves and the fishes, a miracle described in all four synoptic gospels. Above the lintel of the door, the name Patricius is inscribed, the original Latin form of Patrick. Resting on the lintel is the distinctive St. Brigid's Cross made of rushes which symbolises the protection by Ireland's foremost female saint of all who pass through the door.

Once inside the quiet space, the dominant feature of the chapel is the incandescent stained glass window behind the altar. After long searching for a suitable window, University Architect Doug Marsh and Kevin Whelan discovered an original Harry Clarke drawing framed behind the desk of Ken Ryan, the Director of Abbey Stained Glass Studios in Kilmainham. The drawing, commissioned from the Harry Clarke studio, was for a window that was never actually made. Ken Ryan was able to get an experienced craftsman, Kevin Kelly, who had been trained in the Harry Clarke Studios, to make this stunning window.

At the centre of the composition, Our Lady holding the infant Jesus is enthroned on the Seat of Wisdom. Beside her is St. Patrick, the evangeliser of the Irish, holding a model

The Chapel in O'Connell House.

Colm Brennan holds a wax tablet of what became the tabernacle placque.

of the medieval church at Glendalough, and the Bachall Phádraig, his wooden crozier which was venerated at St. Patrick's Cathedral in Dublin until it was destroyed during the Reformation. St. Colmcille, the patron saint of education, is also depicted (Columba Hall across from the Grotto on Notre Dame campus is named in his honour). Among the details portrayed in the window are the crown of the Virgin above the shamrock, an appropriate emblem of the dedication of Ireland to Mary, and St. Patrick's Bell, one of the treasures of the National Museum. The crests of the University of Notre Dame and the Congregation of the Holy Cross are added on panels at each side of the window. These themes dovetail the intertwined histories of Notre Dame and Ireland, and it would be difficult to imagine a more appropriate window for the chapel in O'Connell House.

To the left of the altar is the tabernacle with a bronze relief of the crucified Christ sculpted by Colm Brennan. It is based on a book placque dating from the tenth century. Early Irish manuscripts like the Book of Kells were unbound, and were stored as single sheets in wooden boxes. The outside of the boxes containing revered manuscripts was decorated with metal placques. This particular placque was recovered from the River Shannon by divers and is now displayed in the National Museum. It offers a visual synthesis of the Christian and the Celtic tradition. Christ is shown as an Irish warrior, with the characteristic 'glib', the distinctive Irish male hairstyle. He is also depicted wearing a cloak ornately decorated in the Celtic style. The Irish did not like the idea of Christ being vanquished on the cross so they supply two Celtic angels to hold his head upright – the earliest depiction of this motif in European art. Stephanus and Longinus are shown on either side of the crucified Christ, with the spear, the sponge and the hyssop.

Just under the ceiling, lines from the breastplate of St. Patrick are inscribed in light gold by Tim O'Neill, the most accomplished modern Irish calligrapher. The excerpts are punctuated by Celtic crosses, which are modelled on a tenth-century example from Clonmacnoise monastery. The corpus image of Christ is derived from the tabernacle placque. The shimmering Pentecostal flame hand-stitched on the altar cloth is comprised of ten thousand gold thread stitches by Alexis Von Bernstoff from County Wexford. The Irish oak altar and chairs were made by the O'Driscoll brothers, skilled artisans from County Cork. The twelve ceiling lights are arrayed to mirror the crown of the Blessed Virgin, a fitting symbol of the abiding presence of Notre Dame in O'Connell House.

HARRY CLARKE (1889–1931)

Harry Clarke, designer of the window in the O'Connell House Chapel, has been described as among the greatest post-medieval masters of stained glass, and he also won enduring fame as a book illustrator. Clarke was an absolute master of the Gothic – the Irish writer AE (George Russell) called him 'one of the strangest geniuses of his time'. Clarke was attracted to the medieval combination of the beautiful and the grotesque, the spiritual and the macabre – a tendency intensified by his chronic tuberculosis and his opium addiction. Operating at the limits of technical skill in stained glass, he achieved mastery of colour – vibrant and gem-like in its crystalline brilliance, and yet also ethereal and sumptuous.

While his work stemmed from the intersection of Art Nouveau and Art Deco, Clarke was also Ireland's major Symbolist artist. He was strongly influenced by the Irish Cultural Revival of the late nineteenth and early twentieth century. He is as firmly rooted in the Irish Revival as in European art movements of this period. The Irish Arts and Crafts movement had a public rather than domestic focus – unlike its American and English counterparts. Its highpoint was An Túr Gloine (The Glass Tower), an organisation founded in Dublin in 1903 by the Irish artist Sarah Purser, and dedicated to making exceptional stained glass through artisanal rather than mass production methods.

An Túr Gloine stimulated an efflorescence of Irish stained glass, notably in the work of Harry Clarke, Michael Healy and Evie Hone, that elevated Ireland from a provincial backwater into the heart of modern design. The aim was to replace the anaemic industrially-produced German glass that dominated Victorian Catholic churches. These Irish artists excelled in using acid etching to create a pointillist effect, creating a shimmering hue.

Harry Clarke was the most talented of a gifted generation. He produced more than 130 windows, after taking over his father's studio in 1921. His glass is distinguished by the unusual finesse of its drawing, his love of sumptuous colours (inspired by an early visit to the Cathedral of Chartrès, he was especially attracted to deep blues), and an incorporation of the window leading into the overall designs. Highlights include his superb work for the Honan Chapel in University College Cork, and a magnificent jewel-like treatment of Keats' *The Eve of St. Agnes* (perhaps the single most beautiful art object in Ireland), now

The Harry Clarke window in O'Connell House (detail).

in the Hugh Lane Municipal Gallery in Dublin. He also created the controversial Geneva Window in 1929, brilliantly depicting Irish writers, but too daring for the conservative taste of the time. This Irish masterpiece is now housed in the Wolfsonian Institute in Miami.

The son of a craftsman, Harry Clarke was exposed to art (and in particular Art Nouveau) at an early age. He attended Belvedere College in Dublin and by his late teens, he was studying stained glass at the Dublin Art School, where he won a gold medal in 1910. Although stained glass is central to Clarke's career, he was also a book illustrator of global stature. Clarke travelled to London to work in the book trade. Hans Christian Andersen's *Fairy Tales* appeared in 1916, including sixteen colour plates by Clarke. His colour illustrations for Poe's *Tales of Mystery and Imagination* were published in 1923. A critic opined: 'Never before ... have these marvellous tales been visually interpreted with such flesh-creeping, brain haunting, illusions of horror, terror and the unspeakable'. He followed with celebrated editions of Perrault's *Fairy Tales* and a magnificently terrifying version of Goethe's *Faust* (1925).

These volumes established Clarke's reputation as a world-class book illustrator, even during this golden age of book illustration. His work stands comparison with Aubrey Beardsley, Arthur Rackham and Edmund Dulac. Clarke, plagued by ill health accentuated by the toxic chemicals used in stained glass production, died of tuberculosis in a Swiss sanatorium in 1931.

ND students pray below the flag in St. Peter's Square, Rome.

Climbing Croagh Patrick – Ireland's holy mountain.

CAMPUS MINISTRY

Since 2002, the Dublin Programme was served by four Campus Ministers, all recent Notre Dame alums – but none of these International Men of Ministry came to Dublin with an Irish surname. Recruited and trained by Darrell Paulsen and the Office of Campus Ministry, these exceptional young men – Michael Downs, Adam Kronk, Luke Klopp, Andrew Hoyt – dedicated themselves to the pastoral care of ND students in Europe, making them feel a valued part of the Notre Dame family. These ministers supported the students in their faith lives while in a radically different environment, and guided them in seeing the face of God in their encounters with so many different people.

On a Tuesday night in 2002, Campus Minister Michael Downs stood in Newman Chapel on St. Stephen's Green. There he welcomed the Notre Dame students, who had just descended the eighty-four steps from the Keough Centre at the top of Newman House, and who were now gathered in the first few rows of weathered wooden pews of the adjacent church. The students bowed their heads in prayer. All was still, save for the pop of the radiators and the flicker of the altar candles against the intricate mosaic of the Virgin Mary. There, above the apse of the chapel, she is enthroned as *Sedes Sapientiae*, Our Lady (Notre Dame) Seat of Wisdom.

The historical significance of Newman Chapel resonated deeply for Michael, who had been chosen by the University to help Dublin students engage and strengthen their faith lives during their time in Ireland. On that night, the Dublin Programme started a regular tradition: the Tuesday Evening Mass. This first Eucharist marked the inaugural step of an inspirational pilgrimage that has extended across Europe through the years, spreading from Newman Chapel to St. Peter's Square in Rome, the Camino de Santiago de Compostela, Walsingham, Assisi, Medugorje, Lourdes, Le Mans and Westminster Cathedral.

The journey began in the fall of 2002, after student evaluations consistently expressed a hunger for a deeper spiritual component in their time abroad. An essential part of any Notre Dame undergraduate international experience is the personal and spiritual growth that is stimulated by living in a new environment and encountering a different culture.

At the advent of the programme, the core idea was simple: to help students to become pilgrims rather than tourists; where

Alice Harada and Adriana Taylor playing 'Notre Dame, Our Mother' on the top of Croagh Patrick, Spring 2011.

Fr. Tim Scully, CSC, Fr. Sean McGraw, CSC, and Fr. Lou Delfra, CSC, celebrate Mass on Slane Hill, Keough Naughton Centre Dublin Tenth Anniversary Celebration 2008.

the tourist demands, the pilgrim gives thanks. The initiative gradually embraced Europe – in classrooms, in homeless shelters and schoolyards, in churches both humble and historic, in medieval monasteries, over mountains, and everywhere the students walked together in faith. From his base in Dublin, and with the blessing of the Office of International Studies, Campus Minister Michael Downs began building a network of retreats, liturgies, service, pilgrimages and faith-sharing groups. Rather than transplanting the spirituality of Notre Dame to Europe, the guiding principle of Campus Ministry abroad is to draw on the deep spirituality, tradition, and culture of each European setting to inspire our students, breathing new life into their faith.

The overwhelming student response to Campus Ministry's presence in Europe was proof that something fundamental had been lacking during their time abroad. In Dublin, the ground was particularly fertile. Students in the Dublin Programme have served the poor in Dublin, journeyed on the Camino de Santiago de Compostela in Spain, celebrated Easter Mass with Pope John Paul II and Pope Benedict XVI, meditated on retreat in Glendalough, followed in the arduous footsteps of Saint Patrick up his sacred mountain, attended the Beatifications of Blessed Basil Moreau, CSC, and Blessed Mother Teresa of Calcutta, and the Canonisation of Saint André Bessette, CSC, helped the homeless, sustained a basketball programme in Rathmines, became Friends of

ND students at Máméan pilgrimage site in Connemara, Spring 2010.

the Elderly, painted colourful murals in grey places, tutored refugees – the litany continues to grow.

Community, hospitality, and spirituality are at the centre of the Dublin experience, and the Opening Mass is an important early manifestation of those values. The students bond through participation in the celebration of the Eucharist, occasions enriched by their musical and vocal talents. A random assortment of individuals evolves into a cohesive group that is eagerly anticipating the shared journey ahead.

Almost all participants in the Dublin Programme make their way to Glendalough, a dramatic valley with two pristine lakes, nestled in the heart of the Wicklow Mountains. It is the site of the sixth-century monastery that St. Kevin (an Irish precursor of St. Francis of Assisi) founded. The students meditate on their time abroad, and strengthen their sense of community through hiking, praying, reflecting, sharing, and absorbing the natural beauty and rich spiritual tradition of the valley.

Patrick's statue at Máméan takes on a lifelike character when draped in a Notre Dame flag.

Inspired by the 'Christmas in April' movement in America, the Dublin Programme dedicates an entire day each semester to serving their host city. Over the years, Campus Ministry has given Notre Dame students the opportunity to paint a mural and clean up the surroundings of Dublin primary schools, clear up derelict yards and neighbourhoods in the city, and organised a track and field day for enthusiastic twelve-year olds.

The Notre Dame tradition is to give of oneself until it hurts, and students take this to heart by volunteering in the local community as a means of giving back to the city that welcomes them. Locations include Youth Horizons in Jobstown (a facility for early school leavers), Merchant's Arch (a drug rehabilitation centre), Separated Children's Education Services (a facility that serves young asylum-seekers), Friends of the Elderly (an outreach to isolated senior citizens), St. Louis' National School (basketball programme for elementary school kids) and Fighting Words (a writing centre devoted to children of all ages).

While all these activities and programmes emerged under the umbrella of Campus Ministry, the true core remains the nurturing of relationships. It is the community, the hospitality, and the challenge to become pilgrims on their journey together that continues to inspire and motivate students.

From the Heart: Christopher Rehagen, Dublin Spring 2008

I am a 2009 graduate and a Spring 2008 participant in the Dublin Programme. Currently, I am a seminarian studying for the priesthood for the Congregation of Holy Cross (the religious order that founded and continues to run Notre Dame).

My experience with the Dublin programme impacted my decision to enter the seminary following graduation. Surprisingly, considering how much was going on while I was there, my time in Dublin was one of great spiritual growth for me. I really enjoyed the Tuesday night Mass followed by the trips to Eddie Rocket's. I also enjoyed attending daily Mass at the parish in Blackrock (I lived at the dorms in Blackrock). I attended the 10:00 am daily Mass, which usually had around fifty people in the congregation. 49 were over the age of sixty. Despite this, I grew to love the Mass there. I loved how the Irish people always made me feel welcome. I didn't know them well, but they still greeted me with a smile when I arrived. I also was impressed by how the Irish people prayed for the dead in every single Mass I attended. Their belief in the Resurrection was something I envied and learned from.

Most importantly, my time in Dublin helped me realise how important my faith was to me. For the first time in my life, it wasn't all that easy to attend Mass or set aside time to pray. It wasn't like at Notre Dame where Mass is being celebrated at all hours of the day. And yet, I still had a deep desire to attend Mass and stay in the Church for a few minutes after Mass to sneak in a few prayers or pray the Rosary with the men and women of the parish. It wasn't always easy to roll out of bed after a long night the night before, but it was worth it. In Dublin, I felt God in my life in a special way, and I will always be thankful for it.

As part of the Novitiate experience, my classmates and I don't take formal classes but meet daily for conferences. We spend a good portion of our day in prayer and silence. If I discern that God is calling me to the religious life, I will profess the temporary vows of poverty, chastity and obedience for a period of one year, before then returning to Notre Dame to study theology in preparation for the priesthood. After a period of three to six years in temporary vows, we can petition to make the vows permanent through the profession of final vows. The following year we would then be ordained to the priesthood. It is quite a process, but one that I am comfortable with, as I need the time and experience to grow in my relationship with God and to make sure that God is indeed calling me to religious life.

I can't tell you how many old Dublin memories I recalled as I wrote this. It made me remember just how much I loved my time in Dublin; how much I loved the Irish people and culture, the pubs and the museums, the chance to travel throughout both Ireland and Europe, and most importantly, the people I met, both from Notre Dame and from around the world. It was a great experience and one I would do again in a heartbeat.

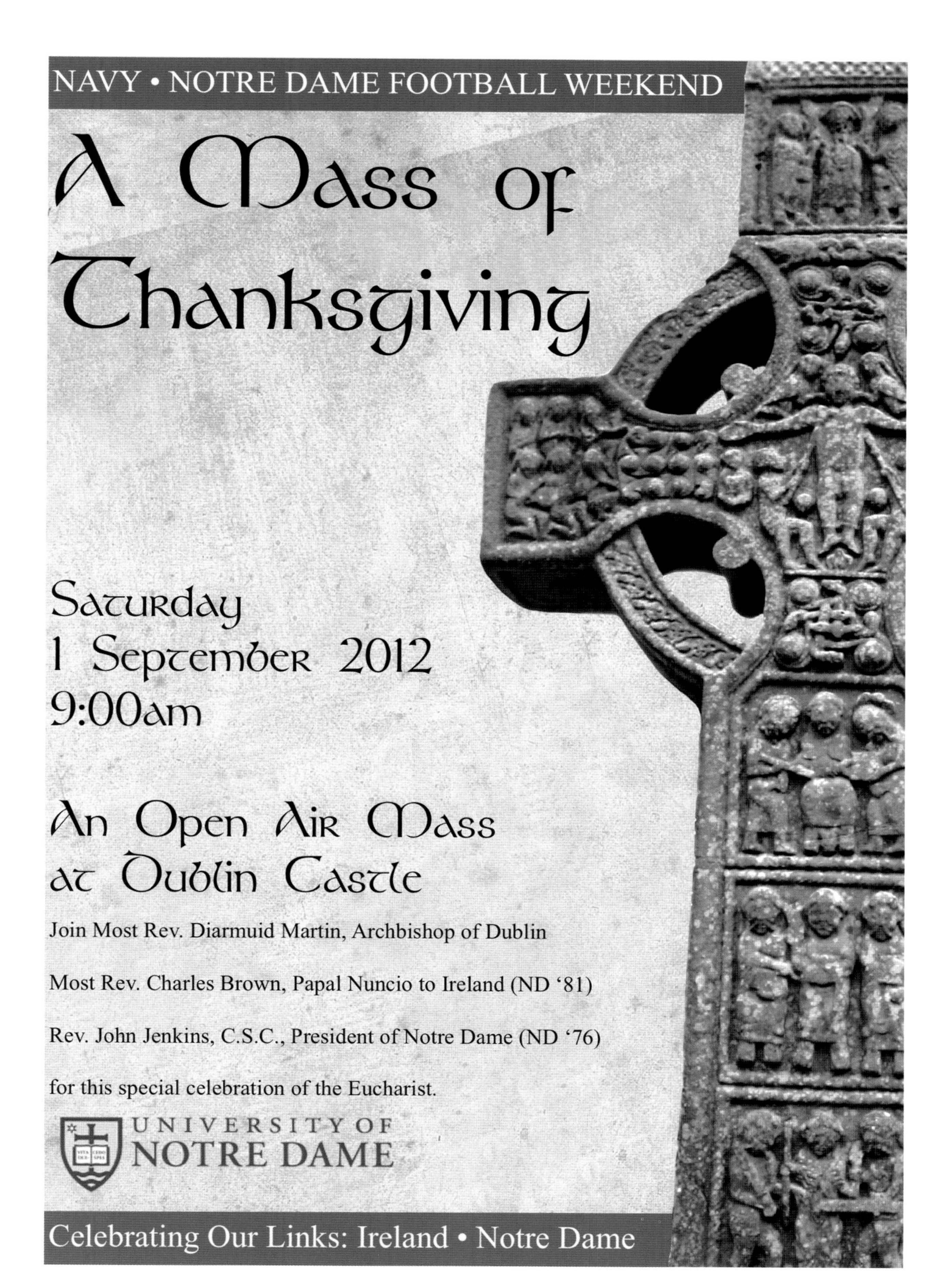
NAVY • NOTRE DAME FOOTBALL WEEKEND
A Mass of Thanksgiving
Saturday
1 September 2012
9:00am
An Open Air Mass at Dublin Castle
Join Most Rev. Diarmuid Martin, Archbishop of Dublin
Most Rev. Charles Brown, Papal Nuncio to Ireland (ND '81)
Rev. John Jenkins, C.S.C., President of Notre Dame (ND '76)
for this special celebration of the Eucharist.
UNIVERSITY OF NOTRE DAME
Celebrating Our Links: Ireland • Notre Dame

NOTRE DAME AND THE CHURCH IN IRELAND

Beyond the involvement of Campus Ministry and its students in the religious, spiritual and cultural life of Dublin, the University of Notre Dame and the Congregation of Holy Cross have been involved in Ireland in a panoply of ways. Ranging from missionary priests, and Catholic Education to liturgical service, these activities have always sought to supplement the Irish Church in a spirit of true partnership.

FR. PATRICK PEYTON, CSC (1909–1992) 'THE ROSARY PRIEST'

Many Irish-born priests joined the ranks of the Congregation of the Holy Cross. Among the most famous was Patrick Peyton, CSC, internationally known as the 'Rosary Priest'. He popularised the famous slogan: 'The family that prays together stays together'. He founded the post-World War II prayer movement called the 'Family Rosary Crusade'. Fr. Peyton staged massive Rosary rallies across the world and extensively utilised mass communication, helped by major Hollywood celebrities, promoting his ministry of binding families through prayer under the Family Rosary. Peyton's charisma inspired Latin America and the Philippines, where he was widely known for his strong Irish accent.

Fr. Peyton was born at Carracastle, County Mayo, the sixth in a family of nine living in a small cabin on a tiny hillside farm. Some of his elder sisters went to America and were sending remittances to help the family left behind. His sisters sent word that Patrick and his older brother Thomas should join them in Scranton, Pennsylvania.

After they arrived there in 1928 and in 1929, both were recruited by the Congregation of Holy Cross. Patrick and Thomas entered the main seminary in Notre Dame in 1932. In 1938, Patrick was diagnosed with TB. His sister Nellie travelled to Notre Dame from Scranton and brought him novenas of the Blessed Mother. Patrick put his health in the hands of the Blessed Virgin Mary and shortly afterwards the doctors discovered that the patches in his lungs had disappeared.

Both brothers were ordained in 1941, as members of the Congregation of Holy Cross. From Albany, New York, Father Peyton's mission started as letters promoting the importance of families praying the Family Rosary. He soon branched out into utilising radio, films, outdoor advertising and later television. Father Peyton was one of the first pioneers of

Fr. Patrick Peyton, CSC.

evangelism using mass media. He also pioneered public rallies to bring families to pledge to pray the Rosary. These Rosary rallies attended by millions became his signature event. He traversed the globe from Brussels to Madrid, across Asia to the Philippines, to New Zealand and Papua New Guinea and into several South American countries. Among Filipino Catholics, Father Peyton is remembered for his Sunday televised shows, where he promoted the Rosary and Marian devotion. He died peacefully holding a Rosary in Los Angeles, California. Cardinal Sean O'Malley announced a formal declaration opening the cause for sainthood of Fr. Peyton in 2001, earning him the revered title of 'Servant of God'.

The Fr. Peyton, CSC, Memorial Centre in Attymass, County Mayo, was dedicated in 1998. The Centre commemorates the life and apostolic work of Fr. Peyton. It is a place of respite, prayer and peace.

Four Dublin ACEr's – Seth Whetzel, Emily Byrne, Don McClure and Kathleen Brogan – with Fr. Tim Scully, CSC, on Inch Strand, County Kerry, in 2006.

ACE ADVOCATES—IRELAND

Founded in 1994, the Alliance for Catholic Education (ACE) at the University of Notre Dame seeks to develop a cadre of highly motivated and committed young educators to meet the needs of the United States most underserved elementary and secondary schools. By recruiting and training recent graduates from top college and universities, ACE serves disadvantaged Catholic primary and secondary schools throughout the USA.

ACE provides an intensive two-year service experience encompassing three pillars – professional development, community life and spiritual growth. Seeking to form leaders in Catholic schools, to prepare informed and active citizens for the world, and to provide high-quality educational opportunities for the underserved, ACE works tirelessly to provide a witness of hope.

Each year, two Irish students are selected to participate in the ACE programme. As part of the wider ACE mission, ACE Advocates Ireland aims to enhance the character of Catholic education both in Ireland and internationally. The Dublin group – the largest one currently in existence – is part of a broad community of ACE Advocates, and is the sole international branch. ACE Advocates wins friends for the mission of Catholic schools, prepares members spiritually and professionally to be agents of change in Catholic education, and mobilises members to have a lasting impact on children, families, communities, the nation and the Church by championing Catholic schools.

ACE Advocates Dublin visit ND campus: here they are greeted by CSC priests Fr. Ted Hesburgh, Fr. Tim Scully, Fr. Sean McGraw, and Fr. Lou Delfra.

Comprised of ACE Alumni, Irish educators, and those passionate about Catholic education, ACE Advocates seeks to be of service to Catholic education in Ireland by: identifying, motivating and developing leaders committed to the character of Irish Catholic schools; supporting the faith life of Irish educators in their teaching, community building and spirituality; building partnerships between educational leaders in the United States and Ireland through our respective experiences of Catholic education.

Teach Bhríde community at O'Connell House: Carolyn Pirtle, Jessica Mannen, Clarisa Ramos, Patrick Duffy.

TEACH BHRÍDE/HOUSE OF BRIGID

The University of Notre Dame Folk Choir, founded in 1980, has been touring Ireland for more than a generation, under the inspiring leadership of Steve Warner. They have undertaken Irish tours in 1988, 1990, 1992, 1994, 1997, 2000, 2003, 2004, 2008 and 2012. Indeed, their 1988 Ireland Tour was the first international expedition undertaken by a liturgical choir from Notre Dame. They have offered concerts all over the land, from St. Patrick's in Armagh to the shores of Galway Bay and Connemara, and they have sung in almost one hundred different churches all over the island. They were the first choir to learn the new sacred music of the Irish and to bring it back to the States, where it was then shared with thousands of faith communities.

The ND Folk Choir playing a concert in the National Concert Hall Dublin in 2012.

In 2008, the Notre Dame Folk Choir decided to create a bold new initiative: an intentional lay community, dedicated to inspiring the young people of Ireland. Notre Dame graduates experience the life-giving impact of immersion in a joyful and tangible expression of their faith. It is one of the great strengths of the University. The Folk Choir wanted to take that experience and to use it to invite other young men and women deeper into their faith tradition.

The Folk Choir named their Irish initiative Teach Bhríde – The House of Brigid. They chose as their beachhead the town of Wexford, which has an intimate connection with the Folk Choir. One parish in particular, the Church of the Annunciation in Clonard, had all the right ingredients for the new community: an energetic and hospitable pastor and curates (Monsignor Denis Lennon, Fr. Martin Doyle, Fr. Sean Devereux), a supportive bishop, a parish council that was willing to embrace the programme, a parish centre ideal for church gatherings, and an already-formed group of musicians, receptive to new ideas.

In 2009, the first team of Folk Choir graduates arrived in the parish to begin their work. That pioneering group of Teach Bhríde Volunteer Ministers comprised Chris Labadie, Carolyn Pirtle and Martha Calcutt. In 2010-2011, the community was Carolyn Pirtle, Jessica Mannen, Clarisa Ramos and Patrick Duffy. They were followed in 2011-2012 by Jessica Mannen, Molly Mattingly, Daniel Masterton and Kurt Nowak.

The community helps create new choirs, assists with sacramental preparation, provides uplifting musical and liturgical experiences in the grade schools, and serves as a diocesan resource for liturgical music workshops. The community also supplies a supportive ministry to ACE Advocates-Ireland and the students of the Keough Naughton Notre Dame Centre. Monthly celebrations of the Eucharist for Notre Dame students and staff, along with special annual services (like Thanksgiving and St. Patrick's Day liturgies) are communal events at which the House of Brigid provides superb sacred music.

As their reputation spread, they have also been invited to other parishes and dioceses – some as far away as Galway. Most Rev. Denis Brennan, Bishop of Ferns, lauds their positive impact: 'They have come to serve the parish and the diocese through the Ministry of Music, Liturgical Renewal, Youth Activities and Catechesis. I thank God for their presence. I salute and thank their families for facilitating and supporting this new and exciting venture in our diocese'.

From the Heart: Betsy McGovern, Dublin Fall 2011

Now that I am back on the beautiful ND campus, I am thrilled to be starting classes and meeting up with friends. It's fantastic to be back at South Dining hall with its endless amounts of food!! But I still miss Dublin and OCH – all of you were incredibly instrumental in making my experience in Ireland picture perfect. The transition from ND to Dublin was a piece of cake, thanks to your hard work and commitment to making OCH a home away from home. No other abroad program has what OCH offers. A close friend who goes to Boston College is studying abroad in Dublin – I kept asking about who was picking her up from the airport and helping her with luggage – they have no Joe Stranix! Visiting ND students and family praise what us 'Dublin Domers' got from OCH. The OCH is such a special place and I am so grateful to have had it during my time in Ireland. All of the staff and students became one big Dublin family – thank you so much for all the incredible memories. Go raibh maith agaibh.

From the Heart: Diana Gutierrez, Dublin Summer Programme 2012

There's a moment when a place becomes a home. Not just a house, not just a living space, but an actual home. When a neighbourhood becomes more than just houses on a street, and storefronts with shiny things. When a nation ceases to be just lines on a map and instead becomes something more. Something closer to the heart, a home. It is a moment of pure emotion, of taking in all that's around you and committing it not just to mental memory, but to emotional memory. Allowing it to lodge within yourself, within your heart to be forever unforgotten.

I am not entirely certain whether that moment occurred while strolling down Grafton Street, during one of our many day trips, during our quiet moments at the Giants' Causeway or the Hook peninsula, or in the Burren surrounded by wild flowers and orchids, or during the Celtic Twilight concert high up in an ancient castle. However I am certain that it did in fact occur, that Dublin, and Ireland itself, has become yet another home, another place to miss, for me.

Throughout my time in Ireland, I learned more and more about the country and the city through the classes, but equally through our various activities and trips. Ireland to me was a combination of two worlds, modern and ancient that fused to create a unique culture. The programme allowed us to experience both, to view the past through the present and to see its effects on everyday life. The history of Ireland remained alive: the emigration of thousands, the struggle for independence, the Celtic Tiger – all left their mark on the city and its people. The island had an aura that seeped into one's bones. In comparison, the United States seems so young and its history less valued. Ireland carries its history not in a crippling manner, but in a way that fuels its fire, its future.

To me Ireland is reminiscent of my native Mexico and its history. Both are sources of waves of emigration, both share histories of revolution and the republic. They both take pride in their nationality, their history and their people. I had intuited this association between Ireland and Mexico before my journey, but my time in Dublin solidified it and made it easier to simply fall in love with Ireland.

My experience was everything that I expected, yet nothing I could ever have imagined previously. The culture, the song, the dance, the poetry, the gardens, the parks, the shops, the pubs, the people, captured my heart. Now a piece of me will also miss the green and grey, the Atlantic and the Burren, Newgrange and Wexford. My only regret was having to leave so soon. I can only hope to return again one day to yet another of my homes: Mexico, Notre Dame, Ireland.

Keough Naughton Notre Dame Centre Dublin, Tenth Anniversary 2008

Somos ND
I am my brother's and sister's keeper
WE ARE ND

IRISH

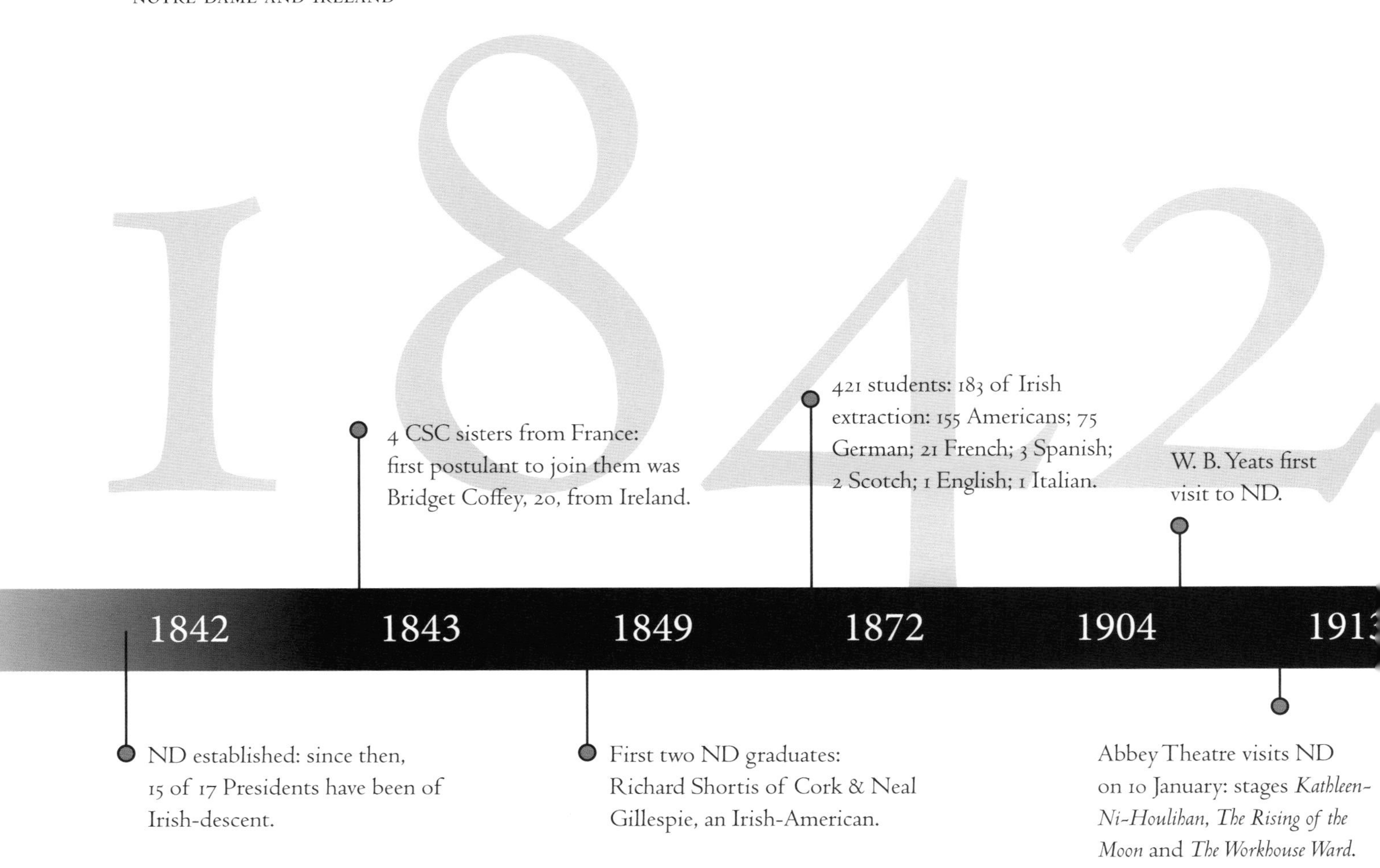
1842
1842
ND established: since then, 15 of 17 Presidents have been of Irish-descent.
1843
4 CSC sisters from France: first postulant to join them was Bridget Coffey, 20, from Ireland.
1849
First two ND graduates: Richard Shortis of Cork & Neal Gillespie, an Irish-American.
1872
421 students: 183 of Irish extraction: 155 Americans; 75 German; 21 French; 3 Spanish; 2 Scotch; 1 English; 1 Italian.
1904
W. B. Yeats first visit to ND.
Abbey Theatre visits ND on 10 January: stages Kathleen-Ni-Houlihan, The Rising of the Moon and The Workhouse Ward.

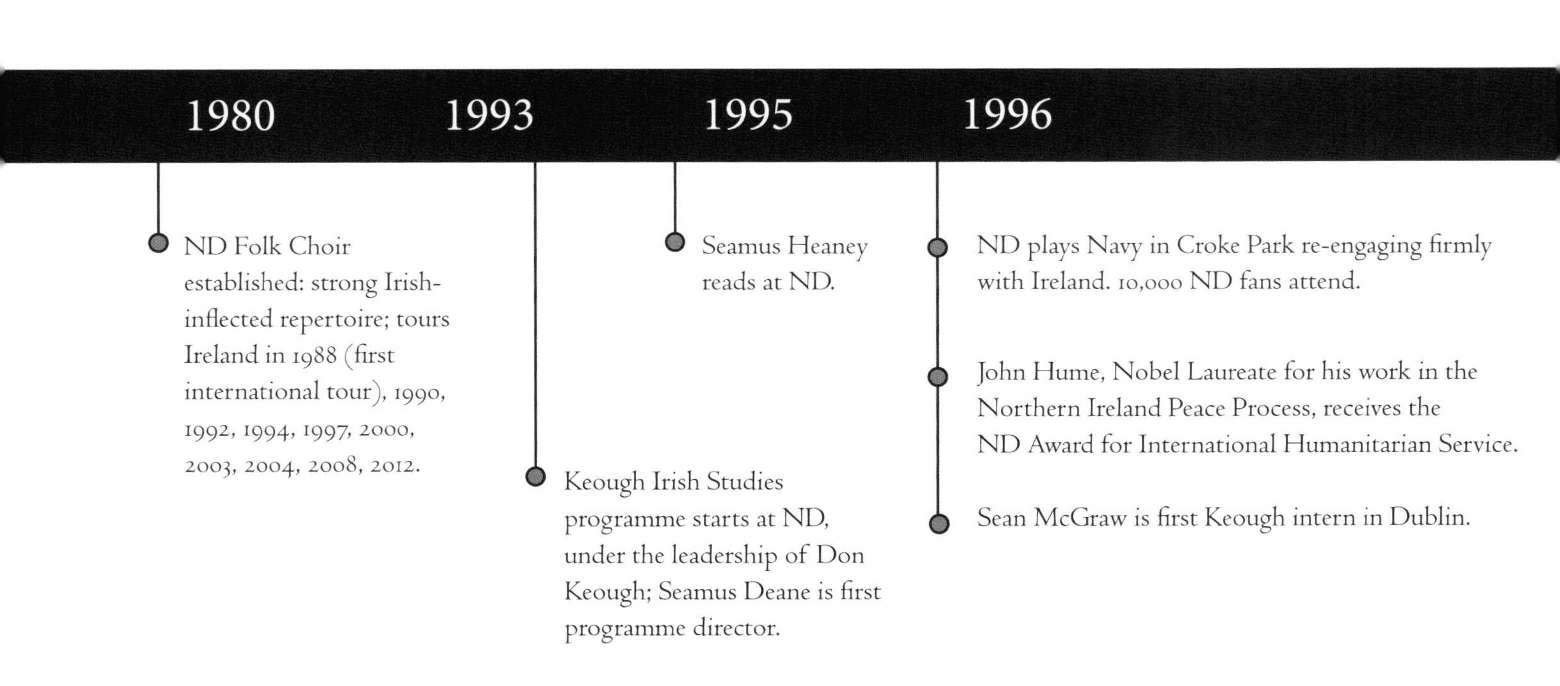
1980
ND Folk Choir established: strong Irish-inflected repertoire; tours Ireland in 1988 (first international tour), 1990, 1992, 1994, 1997, 2000, 2003, 2004, 2008, 2012.
1993
Keough Irish Studies programme starts at ND, under the leadership of Don Keough; Seamus Deane is first programme director.
1995
Seamus Heaney reads at ND.
1996
ND plays Navy in Croke Park re-engaging firmly with Ireland. 10,000 ND fans attend.
John Hume, Nobel Laureate for his work in the Northern Ireland Peace Process, receives the ND Award for International Humanitarian Service.
Sean McGraw is first Keough intern in Dublin.

919

Éamon De Valera, first President of the Irish Republic, arrives at ND on 15 October.

1920s

ND sports teams nicknamed the 'Fighting Irish'; ND wins College Football National Championships in 1924, 1929 & 1930.

1933

Count John McCormack, Irish tenor, receives the Laetare medal.

W. B. Yeats' second visit to ND.

1935–41

Desmond Fitzgerald, veteran of the 1916 Rising and former Irish government minister, lectures in philosophy at ND.

1953

1953: *The Vanishing Irish*, a collection of essays on Irish emigration patterns since the Famine, edited by Fr John O'Brien, CSC of ND.

1968

President Éamon de Valera hosts the ND Rugby Team at Áras an Uachtaráin.

1998

ND's Ireland Programme starts on 17 October at Newman House on Stephens Green. Kevin Whelan is appointed inaugural Michael J. Smurfit Director.

1999

ND establishes Ireland Council under chairs Don Keough and Martin Naughton.

Inaugural Irish Seminar held in Dublin: founded by Christopher Fox and Kevin Whelan.

PHOTO CREDITS

Eimear Clowry 12, 14, 16, 17, 33, 34, 35, 40, 54, 55, 57, 61, 62, 67, 69, 70, 71, 75, 78, 81, 83, 87, 94, 100, 101, 103, 104, 105, 106, 107, 109, 110, 112, 114, 115, 118, 119, 121, 122, 123, 124, 125, 128, 129, 131, 134, 136, 137, 142, 143

Keough Naughton Centre 45, 67, 77, 79, 80, 90, 93, 94, 99, 116, 130, 131, 139

Edmund Ross 6, 22, 24, 25, 26, 31, 65, 74, 82, 96, 112, 113, 124, 133, 145

Matt Cashore 8, 27, 38, 53, 56

Courtney Wahle 17, 81, 102, 109

Notre Dame Archives 39, 46, 49

Aoife Drinan 10, 11, 19

Andrew Hoyt 109, 133, 136

Eoghan Kavanagh, Skyline Gallery, 72, 73

Keough Naughton Centre, © Seamus Heaney 84, 85

Elizabeth Moore 88, 89

Donal Murphy 20-21

Máire Devlin 9

TCD 13

Brendan Dunford 15

Molly Byrne 18

Nile's Magazine 28

Russ A. Pritchard jr 42

Abbey Theatre 47

Irish Photo Archive 50

Greer Hannan 52

Ó Buachalla Family 63

Rachael Naughton 65

Mary & John Lesch Family Collection 68

Jane Bown 82

Chicago Art Institute 94

Monica Bushman 107

Elena Rodriguez 110

Kevin Whelan 126

Luke Klopp 135

Siomha Moore 135

Carolyn Bates 137

Family Rosary International 140

Alliance for Catholic Education 141

Colleen McCartney 146

Kate Nolan 86

Louise Marren 122

South Bend Tribune 51

University College Dublin 51

Victor Patterson 60

Lisa Caulfield 91

Perry McIntyre 117

Ryan Greenberg 111